POLITICS AND RELIGION

THE BASICS

Politics and Religion: The Basics provides a concise introduction to the complex interactions between politics and religion in both domestic and international contexts.

This book examines the role of religion in shaping political systems, behaviours and debates worldwide. By introducing some of the most prominent religions, it explores their impact on contemporary politics and sheds light on key topics such as religious nationalism, gender inequality, religious terrorism and the struggle for religious freedom. Using case studies from countries including Iran, the USA, France, China and Turkey, it highlights pivotal events such as Iran's 1979 revolution and addresses modern controversies such as the rise of religious nationalism. Broader discussions on democratisation, globalisation and secularisation are integrated with theoretical insights and practical examples, offering a comprehensive overview of the field.

Aimed at undergraduate students in political science, international relations and religious studies, this book is also a valuable source for scholars. With its clear structure and real-world relevance, it provides an ideal starting point for understanding the dynamic relationship between politics and religion.

ey Haynes is Emeritus Professor of Politics at London opolitan University, UK. His recent edited handbooks le: *Religion and Political Parties* (2019), *Religion, Politics, and 'y* (2021), *Religion and Politics*, 3rd ed. (2023), *Religion & alism* (2025) and *Politics and Religion in Contemporary America* Haynes has written extensively about politics in Ghana in

Christian Nationalism and Democracy in Ghana (2025) and *Revolution and Democracy in Ghana: The Politics of Jerry John Rawlings* (2023). He has also written extensively about religion and politics in the USA, including two research monographs – *From Huntington to Trump: Thirty Years of the Clash of Civilizations* (2019) and *Trump and the Politics of Neo-Nationalism: The Christian Right and Secular Nationalism in America* (2021).

The Basics Series

The Basics is a highly successful series of accessible guidebooks which provide an overview of the fundamental principles of a subject area in a jargon-free and undaunting format.

Intended for students approaching a subject for the first time, the books both introduce the essentials of a subject and provide an ideal springboard for further study. With over 50 titles spanning subjects from artificial intelligence (AI) to women's studies, *The Basics* are an ideal starting point for students seeking to understand a subject area.

Each text comes with recommendations for further study and gradually introduces the complexities and nuances within a subject.

BAYESIAN STATISTICS
THOMAS J. FAULKENBERRY

FAT STUDIES
MAY FRIEDMAN

PROPAGANDA
NATHAN CRICK

THE HUMAN SKELETON
STEVEN N. BYERS

TRANSACTIONAL ANALYSIS
MARK WIDDOWSON

POLITICS AND RELIGION
JEFFREY HAYNES

For more information about this series, please visit: www.routledge.com/The-Basics/book-series/B

POLITICS AND RELIGION

THE BASICS

Jeffrey Haynes

LONDON AND NEW YORK

Designed cover image: © Getty Images

First published 2026
by Routledge
4 Park Square, Milton Park, Abingdon, Oxon OX14 4RN

and by Routledge
605 Third Avenue, New York, NY 10158

Routledge is an imprint of the Taylor & Francis Group, an informa business

© 2026 Jeffrey Haynes

The right of Jeffrey Haynes to be identified as author of this work has been asserted in accordance with sections 77 and 78 of the Copyright, Designs and Patents Act 1988.

All rights reserved. No part of this book may be reprinted or reproduced or utilised in any form or by any electronic, mechanical, or other means, now known or hereafter invented, including photocopying and recording, or in any information storage or retrieval system, without permission in writing from the publishers.

Trademark notice: Product or corporate names may be trademarks or registered trademarks, and are used only for identification and explanation without intent to infringe.

British Library Cataloguing-in-Publication Data
A catalogue record for this book is available from the British Library

ISBN: 978-1-032-83333-0 (hbk)
ISBN: 978-1-032-82688-2 (pbk)
ISBN: 978-1-003-50882-3 (ebk)

DOI: 10.4324/9781003508823

Typeset in Bembo
by Newgen Publishing UK

To my wife, Bodhilehi, a consistent and profound source of encouragement for my academic and scholarly writings.

CONTENTS

1 The basics   1

Introduction 1
Politics and religion: Modernisation and secularisation 3
What the book is about 5
Politics 6
Religion 8
World Religions: Buddhism, Christianity,
* Confucianism, Hinduism, Islam and Judaism 10*
The book: Chapter by chapter 17
Conclusion 20

2 Domestic politics   23

State and religion 23
Political society 32
Civil society 35
Social capital 39
Conclusions 42
Questions 42

3 International politics — 46

Globalisation and religion 51
International politics and religion 55
Post-secular international politics 58
Conclusion 61
Questions 63

4 Contentious politics — 66

Contentious politics and religion 67
Democratisation and democracy 71
Right-wing populism 74
Culture wars 77
Religious terrorism 81
Conclusion 85
Questions 86

5 Gender and feminism — 90

Gender and politics 90
Gender, power and ideology 92
Islamic feminism 98
Turkey and Islamic feminism 102
France and Islamic feminism 104
Conclusion 107
Questions 108

6 Freedom and discrimination — 112

State policies with respect to freedom of religion or belief 112
International religious freedom after World War II 116
State discrimination against religious minorities in the Middle East and North Africa 118
International discrimination against women and sexual minorities 122
Discrimination against the non-religious in sub-Saharan Africa 125
Conclusion 130
Questions 131

7 Nation and nationalism 135

Secular nationalism 135
Nationalism and religion 139
Nationalism and Confucianism 144
Nationalism and Christianity 145
Nationalism and Islam 148
Conclusion 151
Questions 152

8 Challenges and opportunities 156

Politics, religion and security 158
Politics, religion, governance and global order 164
Conclusion 167

Index 170

THE BASICS

> **INTRODUCTORY BOX : RELIGION AND POLITICS**
>
> Many of us have a good idea what comprises 'politics' and many of us think we would recognise 'religion' if we saw it. Let's start with the following, before going into the issue in a bit more depth later. Let's assume that 'politics' is about who gets power and what they do with it. 'Religion' is often, but not always, about human faith in a god or gods. Yet, some religions, notably Buddhism and Confucianism, do not have a god, while Hinduism has a great many. Two key questions to get the thought processes going:
>
> - *Why* do politics and religion frequently interact?
> - *What happens* when there is a clear and sustained relationship between politics and religion?

INTRODUCTION

The study of religion and politics represents an important subfield of research in political science and international politics. Their importance has grown in recent decades due to increasing interactions between various religious entities and governments and other aspects of the state, amounting to a significant national and global role.

Some regard the study of religion and politics as a difficult area of inquiry due to the presumed complexity of their interrelationship.

DOI: 10.4324/9781003508823-1

The purpose of this book is to make things simple but not simplistic. The book seeks to clarify relevant issues for the reader, especially those encountering the study of religion and politics for the first time, perhaps during introductory university studies. The book is primarily aimed at entry-level undergraduate students encountering the topic of 'religion and politics' during initial studies and should also be useful as the student advances through intermediary-level engagement with relevant subjects.

In short, if you want to know more about the relationship between religion and politics, this book is for you. It presupposes very little prior knowledge of either topic. It aims to inform and educate in an accessible way. Let's get going!

The first thing to be aware of is that the relationship between religion and politics is multifaceted; that is, it has many different aspects. The purpose of this book is to explain this multifaceted relationship in both domestic and international settings, in relation to a number of countries, chosen as case studies because of their identifiable religious and political characteristics. Overall, my aim is to make the relationship between politics and religion and clear and understandable.

Second, we are looking at the issue because interactions of politics and religion have significant impacts on events and outcomes in the 'real' world. If we want to understand what is going on, we cannot afford to ignore what happens when politics and religion meet.

Third, from the Americas to Europe, from the Middle East to Africa and Asia, religion is an important factor in politics, including in relation to political activity and organisation.

BOX 1.1 POLITICS AND RELIGION AFTER WORLD WAR II

The background to today's relationship between politics and religion can be dated back to the years after World War II ended in 1945. At the time, the issue of politics and religion was of rather minor concern for policy makers and political science and international politics scholars and students. The 1930s had been a time of competing secular ideologies, that is, ideologies with no important role for religion, including fascism, communism and liberal

> democracy. After the wartime defeat of Nazi Germany and Imperial Japan, world politics focused on cooperation, seeking to ensure that a cataclysm such as World War II never happened again. The United Nations (UN) organisation was created as a focal point to apply collective state energy to the business of building peace and cooperation. Religion was not a feature of the UN, nor were religious leaders or organisations given places of influence in the new organisation.

Today, religion's social and political significance and influence is universal. While its impact varies from country to country and international context, religion is now much more consistently sociopolitically significant today compared to 50 or 60 years ago. How and why is religion now politically 'significant'? It is largely because religion encourages, or helps resolve, political, social, economic and developmental competition and conflicts. Religion has important functions, serving to engender and/or significantly influence individual and group values. The outcome may be societal conflict within countries, which may spill over to become regional or international security concerns (for a survey, see Haynes 2023).

POLITICS AND RELIGION: MODERNISATION AND SECULARISATION

The first post-war task was to rebuild war-shattered societies and economies. Following World War II, the Western democratic countries in Europe, North America, Australia and New Zealand experienced a new era of political party formation. Democracy was in favour, and the West sought to use its power and influence to spread democracy worldwide.

The world witnessed a 'wave' of democratisation from the mid-1970s, leading to the overthrow of many undemocratic regimes, replaced by governments chosen by the votes of citizens. As countries democratised, religious organisations were often active participants in civil society and began to make their views felt on political and social issues. In addition, some countries had political parties with religious foundations, such as Christian Democratic parties in some European countries, while countries in the Middle East and North Africa saw the emergence of parties whose ideology was political Islam; they are known as 'Islamist' parties.

As a result of religion's growing political presence, politics around the world was influenced by religious organisations, which focused on issues which they believed to be important. Political science and the study of international politics were compelled to take religion seriously in their analyses because of the significant role that religion has played in politics around the world in recent decades. Over time, the scope of inquiry of religion and politics expanded to encompass the complexity and multiplicity of forms whereby they interact. Today, in both the West and the global south, there is increased interaction of religion and politics, helping shape many countries' political direction and outcomes. Today, the interaction of religion and politics drives scholarly research and policy interest in many areas, including democracy, gender, nationalism and populism. We look at these issues, and many others, in the remaining chapters of the book.

A sustained focus on interactions between politics and religion encouraged political scientists and international politics analysts to assess the ability of religion to influence political outcomes in both 'developed' and 'underdeveloped' countries. For many scholars, the status of 'developed' or 'underdeveloped' depended on the degree of 'modernisation' in a country. For many, modernisation was characterised by secularisation, a process leading to a consistent decline in religion's public importance. Secularisation implied that modernised societies were necessarily secular societies. Western countries, with the notable exception of the United States of America, are characterised as secular, with little or no public role for religion. Secularisation was seen as a consequence of the West's trajectory of both industrialisation and urbanisation during the late 19th and 20th centuries.

The Iranian revolution of 1979 was a wake-up call to scholars, analysts and policy makers who believed that the public importance of religion was bound to decline significantly as modernisation progressed. Iran's revolution was led by religious scholars and activists. It demonstrated that Iran, despite significant modernisation, was a country where religion fuelled a revolution whose outcome was the ousting of a pro-Western ruler whose political demise was regarded with alarm in Washington, London and Paris. Now, nearly half a century later, the outcome of Iran's revolution – a theocratic state – remains a key example of the long-term power of religion definitively to shape political outcomes. There are only a few theocratic regimes in the world today. Iran is one, Saudi Arabia is another, Afghanistan is a third – and that's about it. What they have in common is a system of government led by religious figures who claim to rule in the name of God.

Iran's revolution fundamentally challenged the tenets of what is known as secularisation theory. Prior to Iran's revolution, the study of religion and politics was moulded by expectations that as a country modernised, that is, urbanised, industrialised, and with increasingly high levels of citizen education, religion would lose its once important public and political role. This was known as secularisation theory and it was so widely accepted that many scholars regarded as one of the few 'laws' of the social sciences. The position today is that while secularisation is continuing in many countries, notably in Western Europe, as well as in Australia, Canada and New Zealand, in others, including the USA and most countries in the global south, secularisation is progressing more slowly and, as a result, religion continues to have a prominent public role (Norris and Inglehart 2004). That is, in many countries, religion continues to command the attention and loyalty of vast numbers of people and has important, continuing effects on political outcomes.

WHAT THE BOOK IS ABOUT

The book identifies and examines important issues central to our understanding of what happens when politics meets religion in both national and international contexts. We start from the observation that for billions of people around the world their religion is the most important signifier of their identity. This significantly affects many people's perceptions of their identity, society and governance. At the same time, religion does not act in isolation, and in recent years, two key developments led to increased religious responses to political concerns in many parts of the world.

On the one hand, the widespread expansion – and more recently decline – in numbers of democratically elected governments provide space for religion to be publicly prominent and to impact on various political and social issues.[1] On the other hand, because religion is so fundamental to many people's identity, opening political and social space often encourages new or pre-existing tensions to surface or resurface, leading in some cases too hard to resolve, sometimes intractable, inter-group conflicts (Haynes 2023).

Collectively, the chapters of this book emphasise the following:

- Politically assertive religion impacts upon governance and security outcomes within many countries, as well as internationally.
- Globalisation and associated technology, including satellite television channels and social media, play an important role in spreading sectarian and interfaith mistrust.
- Factionalism within religious traditions exacerbates societal tensions, both within countries and internationally.
- High levels of economic and developmental inequality – often linked to religious, ethnic and/or class divisions – are significant sources of national, regional and international competition and sometimes conflict.
- Sectarian and other inter-religious tensions frequently reflect longstanding socio-economic disparities which can escalate, leading to political conflicts when governments fail adequately to deal with them.

Before going further, let's define and explain some key terms.

POLITICS

A political sociologist, Professor Christina Boswell (2020), notes that when we refer to something as being 'political', or 'all about politics', we are generally referring to power struggles between individuals or groups. This implies that politics is 'a process of manoeuvring to assert rival interests'. Of course, this notion of competition over interests or power is very relevant to politics with a capital 'P', or party politics. Indeed, we might start by defining politics as a process of competitive claims-making by rival parties, with the aim of mobilising support to put these programmes into action. But beyond this broad definition, it's useful to unpack what this competition is about and the way in which it plays out. Both of these questions will help us develop a rather more nuanced (and hopefully less cynical!) view of politics.

First, what is politics *about*? One of the classic answers to this question is, according to the British political scientist, Harold Lasswell (1936), that politics is about who gets what, when and how. This suggests that politics is essentially about settling contestation over the distribution of material goods. This may have been a fair characterisation of politics in the post-World War II era – an era that saw the rolling out of progressive taxation and welfare provision by a relatively centralised state and a party-political system based on a traditional left-right ideological cleavage.

Yet the notion that politics is solely, or mainly, about distribution has been challenged over the past three or more decades. The increasing salience of what is sometimes called 'post-ideological' contestation around values and lifestyles suggests that politics is as much, or arguably more, about identity and culture as it is about material resources. Much of our contemporary political debate revolves around issues that are not neatly categorised as left or right, such as the environment, gender and sexual rights, immigration and security (Boswell 2020).

To try to bring together political and religious spheres in all their varied aspects and then to discern significant patterns and trends is not a simple task. But, in attempting it, three points are worth emphasising. First, there is something of a distinction to be drawn between looking at the relationship in terms of the impact of religion on politics, and that of politics on religion. At the same time, they are interactive; the effects of one stimulate and are stimulated by the other. In other words, because we are concerned with the way in which power is exercised within societies, and the way(s) in which religion is involved, the relationship between religion and politics is both dialectical and interactive, with each shaping and influencing the other. Both causal directions need to be held in view when seeking to assess the outcomes of the interactions of religion and politics.

Second, religions are creative and constantly changing; consequently, their relationships with politics also vary over time. Associations between religion and secular power may suddenly change. For example, to name just three examples, in Eastern Europe, Latin America, and Iran in recent times, leading religious institutions and figures shifted – apparently abruptly – from support to opposition of incumbent regimes.

Finally, religious organisations as political actors can only be usefully discussed in terms of specific contexts. For many political scientists and international politics specialists, religious interactions with the state are a fruitful area of inquiry. This is a theoretical construct suggested by much of the literature on state-society relations, built on the understanding that religion's specific role is largely determined by a broader context. The assumption is that there is an essential core element of religion shaping behaviour in, for example, Christian, Islamic or Buddhist societies. I question this assumption in the chapters which follow. The focus of many earlier studies has been to seek to analyse how an existing religious belief or affiliation affects political action. In this book, however, we are equally concerned with the reverse process: how specific political contexts affect religion, including religious organisations.

RELIGION

For many people, religion is a – or perhaps, the – central component of what it means to be human. A prominent American political scientist, Jack Snyder (2011), believes that 'Religion is one of the basic forces of the social universe, not just an "omitted variable."' The late Samuel Huntington (1996: 27), also a prominent political scientist, believes that 'In the modern world, religion is central, perhaps *the* central, force that motivates and mobilizes people....'

That seems clear enough ... but, wait a minute, what *is* religion? *Defining* religion satisfactorily is a very difficult, and some would say impossible, task (Fitzgerald 2011). Martin Marty (Marty and Moore 2000: 11–14), a prominent American religious scholar who has written extensively on religion in the United States, begins his discussion of religion by listing 17 different definitions, before commenting that 'Scholars will never agree on the definition of religion.' However, to help us out, Marty identifies several 'phenomena that help describe what we're talking about' when discussing religion. Marty lists five features of religion that 'help point to and put boundaries around the term'. Religion

- focuses our 'ultimate concern'
- builds community
- appeals to myth and symbol
- is enforced through rites and ceremonies
- demands certain behaviour from its adherents

From Marty's characteristics of religion, we can see that religion can be thought of as a system of beliefs and practices – often but not necessarily related to an ultimate being, such as God, 'beings', such as gods, and/or the supernatural. Religion is also what is sacred in a society – that is, ultimate beliefs and practices which are inviolate (Acquaviva 1979). For our purposes, religion may be approached (1) from the perspective of a body of ideas and outlooks – that is, as theology and ethical code (2) as a type of formal organisation – that is, the ecclesiastical 'church', or (3) as a social group – that is, religious groups, organisations and movements.

Religion affects the world in two basic ways: by what it *says* and by what it *does*. The former relates to religion's doctrine or theology, the latter to its importance as a social and political phenomenon and mark of identity. This can work through a variety of modes of institutionalisation, including 'church'-state relations, civil society and political society.

It is important to distinguish between religion at the individual and group levels – because only the latter is normally of importance in political science and international politics. At the same time, individual religious figures, such as the head of the Roman Catholic Church, Pope Francis, the Dalai Lama, Tibet's holiest Buddhist figure, and Osama bin Laden, radical Islamist and leader of al Qaeda, killed by the US government in 2011, all have high international profiles. From an individualist perspective, it is useful to think of religion as 'a set of symbolic forms and acts that relates man (sic) to the ultimate conditions of his existence'

(Bellah 1964: 359). This is religion's *private*, spiritual side. We are, however, primarily concerned in this book with *group* religiosity, whose claims and pretensions are nearly always to some degree political. For the American political scientist, Sabrina Ramet (1995: 64), there is no such thing as a religion without consequences for value systems.

Group religiosity is a matter of collective solidarities and intergroup interactions. Sometimes this focuses on cooperation with other groups; sometimes on tension and conflict, concerned either with shared or contested images of the sacred, or on cultural and class concerns. To complicate matters, however, such influences may well operate differently and with 'different temporalities for the same theologically defined religion in different parts of the world' (Moyser 1991: 11).

WORLD RELIGIONS: BUDDHISM, CHRISTIANITY, CONFUCIANISM, HINDUISM, ISLAM AND JUDAISM

It is conventionally agreed that there are six 'world' religions: Buddhism, Christianity, Confucianism, Hinduism, Islam and Judaism. 'World religions' is a category used in the study of religion to differentiate at least six – and in some cases more[2] – religions that are seen not only to have a large number of followers but are also internationally spread, or are influential in the development of global society.

To understand how and why many religious traditions and movements are involved in politics, we need to know a little about the world religions' basic belief systems. This is because religious beliefs inform what political actions religious figures and their organisations undertake. In this section, we note the basic beliefs of the six world religions. Our focus is on these religions because most of the significant actors in contemporary politics are followers of one of these faiths.

There is potential for religions to act politically in ways that increase chances of cooperation, conflict resolution and peace-building. For example, with regard to Islam, 'Islam has a direct impact on the way that peace is conceptualised and the way that conflicts are resolved in Islamic societies, as it embodies and elaborates upon its highest morals, ethical principles and ideals of social harmony …' (Bouta, Kadayifci-Orellana and Abu-Nimer 2005: 11). The Dalai Lama, leader of Tibetan Buddhism living in exile in India as a result of China's takeover of the territory in the 1950s, has remarked that: 'Every religion emphasizes human improvement, love, respect for others, sharing other people's suffering. On these lines, every religion had more or less the same viewpoint and the same goal' (www.spiritualityandpractice.com/book-reviews/excerpts/view/16195). The American scholar of conflict, Marc Gopin (2000: 13), suggests that it is very likely that all religions have developed laws and ideas that provide civilisation with cultural commitments to critical peace-related values. These include: empathy, an openness to and even love for strangers, the suppression of unbridled ego and acquisitiveness, human rights, unilateral gestures of forgiveness and humility, interpersonal repentance and the acceptance of responsibility of past error as a means of reconciliation and the drive for social justice. On the other hand, religious involvement in politics can also characterised by competition and, sometimes, conflict.

Two of the world's major religions – Christianity and Islam – are growing fast. Christianity is growing annually by around 1.47%, implying 30% expansion in followers by 2035. Christianity's current growth is particularly swift in South and East Asia and sub-Saharan Africa. Progress of Islam between 2010 and 2020 was estimated at 1.7% a year, linked mainly to 'high' birth rates among Muslims in Asia, the Middle East and North Africa and Europe, leading to fast growth in followers of Islam. The Pew Research Center (www.pewresearch.org/topic/religion/), an authoritative American research institute, estimates that, on present trends, the global Muslim population will grow by about 35% by 2030, increasing from 1.6 to 2.2 billion. Countries in both sub-Saharan Africa (including Nigeria, Kenya and Tanzania) and Europe (including France and the Netherlands) have growing social and political tensions between followers of Christianity and Islam, and it may be that the swift expansion of these religions over the next two decades will exacerbate such tensions, with significant implications for global security and governance.

BUDDHISM

Buddhism is both a philosophy and moral practice. Its purpose is to work towards the relief of suffering in existence by ridding oneself of desire. In 2020, it was the world's fourth-largest religion, with over 520 million followers, known as Buddhists, who comprise around 7% of the world's population (religionmediacentre.org.uk/factsheets/factsheet-buddhism/). Buddhists are divided into three main schools: Mahayana (56%), Theravada (38%) and Vajrayana (6%). Rather than a religion as such, Buddhism is often regarded as a philosophy based on the teachings of the Buddha, Siddhartha Gautama (in the Sanskrit form, Siddhattha Gotama in the Pāli form). The Buddha lived between approximately 563 and 483 BCE. Buddhism began in India and gradually spread throughout Asia to Central Asia, Tibet, Sri Lanka and South-East Asia, as well as to China, Mongolia, Korea and Japan in East Asia. Several Asian countries have majority Buddhist populations: Thailand (95% Buddhist), Cambodia (90%), Myanmar (88%), Bhutan (75%), Sri Lanka (70%), Tibet (a region of China, 65%), Laos (60%) and Vietnam (55%). Other Asian countries with significant Buddhist populations include Japan (50%) and Taiwan (43%) (www.buddhanet.net/e-learning/history/bstatt10.htm).

While there are very large differences between different Buddhist schools of thought, they all share an overall purpose and aim: to liberate the individual from suffering (*dukkha*). While some interpretations stress stirring the practitioner to the awareness of *anatta* (egolessness, the absence of a permanent or substantial self) and the achievement of enlightenment and Nirvana, others (such as the 'Tathagatagarbha' sutras) promote the idea that the practitioner should seek to purify him/herself of both mental and moral defilements that is a key aspect of the 'worldly self' and as a result break through to an understanding of the indwelling 'Buddha-Principle' ('Buddha-nature'), also termed the 'True Self', and thus become transformed into a Buddha. Other Buddhist interpretations beseech bodhisattvas (that is, enlightened beings who, out of compassion, forgo nirvana [or heaven] in order to save others) for a favourable rebirth. Others, however, do none of these things.

What most, if not all, Buddhist schools do is to encourage followers to undertake both good and wholesome actions, and consequently not do bad and harmful actions.

CHRISTIANITY

Christianity is an Abrahamic monotheistic religion based on the life and teachings of Jesus Christ. It is the world's largest and most widespread religion with roughly 2.4 billion followers, nearly one-third (31.2%) of the world's population. Christianity is found in probably every one of the world's 200 countries. Christianity is the majority religion in Europe, the Americas, as well as some countries in sub-Saharan Africa and Asia.

Christianity is a faith with foundations in the teachings of Jesus, regarded by Christians as the Son of God. Jesus is the second component of a Trinity, comprising: God the Father, Jesus the Son and the Holy Spirit. Christians believe that Jesus' life on earth, his crucifixion, resurrection and subsequent ascension to heaven are signs not only of God's love for humankind but also his forgiveness of human sins. Christianity also includes a belief that through faith in Jesus, individuals may attain salvation and eternal life. These teachings are contained within the Bible, especially the New Testament, although Christians accept also the Old Testament as sacred and authoritative scripture.

The ethics of Christianity draw to a large extent from the Jewish tradition as presented in the Old Testament, notably the Ten Commandments. There is however some difference of interpretation between them as a result of the practice and teachings of Jesus. Christianity can be further defined generally through its concern with the practice of corporate worship and certain rites. These include the use of sacraments – including the traditional seven rites that were instituted by Jesus and recorded in the New Testament and that confer sanctifying grace (the Eastern Orthodox, Roman Catholic and some other Western Christian churches) and in most other Western Christian churches, by two rites: Baptism and the Eucharist, instituted by Jesus to confer sanctifying grace.

CONFUCIANISM

There are approximately 6.1 million followers of Confucianism worldwide. This represents slightly less than 1% of the world's population (www.uri.org/kids/world-religions/confucianism).

Confucianism is a religious and philosophical system that developed from the writings attributed to the Chinese philosopher Confucius (the latinised version of Kung Fu-tzu (that is, Master Kung), who was a teacher in China (*c*. 551–479 BCE). Confucianism focuses mostly upon the relationships between individuals, between individuals and their families, and finally between individuals and general society. Confucianism profoundly influenced the traditional culture of China and countries that came under Chinese influence, including Korea. Confucianism places a high value on learning and stresses family relationships and is the name given by Westerners to a large body of Chinese scholarly works, which the Chinese refer to as 'the scholarly tradition'. Historically, Confucianism has been culturally and politically influential in several East and South-East Asian countries, including China, Hong Kong, Japan, Singapore, Taiwan and Vietnam. It has long been an important influence in Chinese and Chinese-influenced attitudes towards life, suggesting patterns of living and standards of social value, while providing a backdrop to Chinese political theories and institutions. Key teachings are concerned with principles of good conduct, practical wisdom and 'proper' social relationships. Recently, Confucianism has aroused interest among Western scholars because the ideas it represents are widely regarded as an important component of the concept of 'Asian values'. Several Asian countries including China, Korea, Japan and Singapore have cultures strongly influenced by Confucianism.

HINDUISM

There are 1.2 billion Hindus worldwide (15% of the world's population), with about 95% of them being concentrated in India. Hinduism is the Western term for the religious beliefs and practices of the vast majority of people who live in India. One of the oldest living religions in the world, Hinduism is unique among the world's major religions in that it had no single founder but grew over a period of 4,000 years with the religious and cultural movements of the Indian subcontinent. Hinduism is composed of innumerable sects and has no well-defined ecclesiastical organisation. Its two most general features are the caste system and acceptance of the Veda – that is, the oldest and most authoritative Hindu sacred texts, composed in Sanskrit and gathered into four collections – as the most sacred scriptures.

Hinduism's salient characteristics include an ancient mythology, an absence of recorded history (or 'founder'), a cyclical notion of time, a pantheism that infuses divinity into the world around, an immanentist[3] relationship between people and divinity, a priestly class and a tolerance of diverse paths to the ultimate ('god'). Its sacral language is Sanskrit, which came to India about 5,000 years ago along with the Aryans, who came from Central Asia. It is a varied corpus, comprising religion, philosophy and cultural practice that are both indigenous to and prevalent in India. The faith is characterised by a belief in rebirth and a supreme being that can take many forms and types, by the perception that contrasting theories are all aspects of an eternal truth, and by its followers' pursuit of liberation from earthly evils.

Of the total global Hindu population, about 95% live in India. Other countries with a significant Hindu population include: Nepal (22.5 m.), Bangladesh (14.4 m.), Indonesia (4.3 m.), Pakistan (3.3 m.), Sri Lanka (3 m.), Malaysia (1.5 m.), Mauritius (600,000), Bhutan (560,000), Fiji (300,000) and Guyana (270,000). In addition, the Indonesian islands of Bali, Java, Sulawesi, Sumatra and Borneo all have significant native Hindu populations.

ISLAM

Around a quarter of the world's population (24.1%) are followers of Islam. Muslims are the majority in 49 countries, speaking hundreds of languages and with diverse ethnic backgrounds. Like Christians, Muslims are found in probably every country in the world with major populations throughout the Middle East and North Africa, sub-Saharan Africa and some Asian countries.

The origins of Islam are an allegiance to God, articulated by his prophet Mohammed (c. 570–632 CE). Mohammed was born in

Mecca (in present-day Saudi Arabia) and over a period of 23 years received revelations from an angel (Jibreel, or Gabriel), who Mohammed believed was relaying the word of God. For Muslims, Mohammed was the last in the series of prophets, including Abraham, Moses and Jesus, who refined and restated the message of God. After Mohammed's death in 632, Muslims divided into two strands, Shia and Sunni. The Shiites are followers of the caliph (that is, leader of an Islamic polity, regarded as a successor of Mohammed and by tradition always male) Abu Bakr and those who supported Mohammed's closest relative, his son-in-law, Ali ibn Abi Talib. Overall, Shiites place more emphasis on the guiding role of the caliph. The Sunni, on the other hand, is the majority sect within Islam, followers of the *custom* of the caliphate rather than an individual caliph, such as Ali. The Shia-Sunni division still persists, although both share most of the customs of the religion. About 90% of the world's Muslims are Sunni and about 10% Shia.

Shia Muslims and Sunni Muslims share five fundamental beliefs:

- *Shahada* (profession of faith in the uniqueness of Allah and the centrality of Mohammed as his prophet)
- *Salat* (formal worship or prayer)
- *Zakat* (giving of alms for the poor, assessed on all adult Muslims as 2.5% of capital assets once a year)
- *Hajj* (pilgrimage to Mecca, which every Muslim should undertake at least once in their lifetime; the annual hajj takes place during the last 10 days of the 12th lunar month every year)
- *Sawm* (fasting during Ramadan, the holy ninth month of the lunar year)

JUDAISM

As of 2023, the world's core Jewish population (those identifying as Jews above all else) was estimated at 15.2 million, which is approximately 0.2% of the 8 billion worldwide population (www.jpr.org.uk/countries/how-many-jews-in-world). Many but by no means all Jewish people live in Israel.

Judaism is a term with several distinct meanings: (1) the Jews' monotheistic religion, with origins back to Abraham and with spiritual and ethical principles mainly contained in the Hebrew Scriptures and the Talmud; (2) compliance with the Jewish religion's traditional ceremonies and rites; (3) the Jews' religious, cultural and social practices and beliefs and (4) the people or community identified as Jews.

These aspects of Judaism have an essential shared characteristic: belief in one God who created the universe and continues to rule it. The God who created the world revealed himself to the Israelites at Mount Sinai. The content of that revelation makes up the Jewish holy book, the Torah, with God's will for humankind stated in his commandments. In Judaism, a second major concept is that of the covenant, or agreement, between God and the Jewish people. The covenant worked like this: Jews would acknowledge God, agreeing to obey his laws and in turn God would acknowledge the Jews as his 'chosen people'.

Jews believe that goodness and obedience will be rewarded and sin punished by God's judgment after death. Then at the end of times, God will send his Messiah to redeem the Jews and deliver them to their Promised Land. Although all forms of Judaism come from the Torah, Judaism is mainly derived from the rabbinic movement during the first centuries of the Christian era. At the turn of the third-century Christian Era (CE), the rabbis (Jewish sages), produced the *Mishnah*, the earliest document of rabbinic literature.

THE BOOK: CHAPTER BY CHAPTER

Following this introductory chapter, Chapter 2 surveys the key issues that arise within countries when politics interacts with religion. Our starting point is to note that the study of politics and religion represents an important subfield of research in political science which has grown in importance in recent decades. We can date much of this interest to Iran's 1979 revolution. This was an important event, as it demonstrated, contrary to then-conventional political science understanding, that religion can have profound and long-lasting political effects in a modernised country such as Iran. Iran's revolution stimulated a focus on the complexity and multiplicity of forms by which politics and religion interact within countries at various levels of development.

The chapter draws on examples from several countries, including Iran, the United States of America (USA), England, France, India and China. The overall aim is to explain how the state and religion interact in nations with varying cultures, religious traditions and political systems.

Chapter 3 explains that religion's involvement in politics is not confined to issues involving the state within countries. It also extends to international politics. The chapter explains how the political science focus on the study of religion and politics expanded from the domestic to the international arena. This expansion was expressed in terms of geographic extensiveness, from the West to the global south, and was strongly influenced by multifaceted – political, economic, cultural, and ideational – dimensions of globalisation. In addition, in the wake of the third wave of democratisation, there was widespread spread of multi-party elections, as well as increasing political involvement of religious leaders, activists and organisations around the globe.

Examples in the chapter come from various countries, including the USA, Israel and several Muslim-majority countries in the Middle East and North Africa, where *jihadist* groups – that is, militant Islamic movements that are perceived as existentially threatening to the West – are an important political factor.

Chapter 4 examines the issue of religion in relation to contentious politics, that is, topics linked to areas of significant political and social contestation. We look at four issues in some detail in the chapter for two reasons, first, religious involvement is pronounced, and, second, religions have been used in various ways to try to get the outcomes that activists wish to see. The focused upon areas are: Democratisation and democracy, right-wing populism, culture wars and religious terrorism.

Chapter 5 looks at interactions between gender, feminism and religion. In the chapter, we refer to gender to mean socially constructed characteristics of women, men, girls and boys. These characteristics include norms, behaviours and roles associated with being a woman, man, girl or boy, as well as relationships with each other. As a social construct, gender varies from society to society and can change over time. In relation to religion, gender issues generally focus on the relationship between females and males, with the norm being the subservience of the former to the latter. Overall, the chapter focuses on the subservient position of females in relation to world religions and explains how this situation came about and what can be done to overcome it.

To illustrate the concerns of the chapter, we include brief case studies of Women's Sexual and Reproductive Health Rights at the United Nations, Islamic feminism, the exclusion of (the study of) religion in Latin American gender studies, and the religious and social position of females in a Muslim-majority country, Turkey and a Christian-majority country, France.

Chapter 6 surveys state approaches to religious freedom and religious discrimination. The chapter looks at state relations with religious minorities and with the non-religious (also known as religious 'nones'). Such groups may suffer from discriminatory treatment by the state. We examine: State policies with respect to freedom of religion or belief, international religious freedom after World War II, discrimination against religious minorities in the Middle East and North Africa, international religious discrimination against women and sexual minorities at the United Nations and discrimination against the non-religious in sub-Saharan Africa.

Chapter 7 examines the relationship between religion and the nation, which is often unclear and often controversial. Increasingly, political scientists question the view that religion and nationalism are necessarily separate. This became necessary as it was clear that rather than fading away as secularisation theory assumed, religion showed surprising persistence, while deepening religious identities in many countries around the world.

Nationalism was long regarded by most political scientists as a secular entity. Today, this is no longer the case. This is because, in recent years, the phenomenon of religious nationalism has emerged in countries around the world. This chapter surveys the rise of religious nationalism, identifying and examining examples in various countries and regions, including the USA, Ghana, the

Middle East and North Africa, China and Sri Lanka, with a focus on Christianity, Islam, Confucianism and Buddhism.

The chapter is in four sections, looking at the following topics: secular nationalism, religious nationalism, Christian nationalism, and Islam and nationalism.

Chapter 8 concludes the book. It reflects on the issues and topics examined in the preceding chapters and suggests ways in which the study of politics and religion may develop over time.

CONCLUSION

The aim of this book is to examine how politics affects religion and *vice versa*. We start from the following premises:

- *The relationship between politics and religion is rarely clear or straightforward.* On the one hand, religion is often associated with conflict – a notorious example is the al Qaeda attack on the Twin Towers and the Pentagon on 11 September 2001, which immediately killed nearly 3,000 people. On the other hand, religion is also often associated with cooperation – for example, religions working to help deliver the UN's Sustainable Development Goals by 2030.
- *Religion has an important function in engendering and influencing values*, including those linked to politics, which affects government policy within countries and internationally.
- *To understand fully how politics and religion interact, we need to examine interactions between domestic and international spheres.* In other words, it is no longer fruitful – as a result of deepening globalisation – to see the domestic and the international as separate areas of analysis when seeking to gauge the outcomes of interactions between religion and politics.

To end this introductory chapter, here are a few questions to get you thinking:

- What are the connections between religion and politics?
- What happens when religion and politics interact?

- Do these connections differ from place to place or are they the same everywhere?
- Is religion becoming more or less politically important?

NOTES

1 The journal, *Democratization*, which the present author co-edits, is a leading scholarly focus on democratisation and its recent decline. See past issues at www.tandfonline.com/journals/fdem20
2 For example, some would include other religions, such as Sikhism and Shinto, in the list of world religions.
3 Immanentism refers to something existing in the realm of the material universe and/or human consciousness.

REFERENCES

Acquaviva, Sabino. 1979. *The Decline of the Sacred in Industrial Society*. Oxford: Blackwell.

Bellah, Robert. 1964. 'Religious evolution', *American Sociological Review*, 29: 358–74.

Boswell, Christina. 2020. *What is Politics?*, The British Academy. www.thebritishacademy.ac.uk/blog/what-is-politics/

Bouta, Tsjeard, S. Ayse Kadayifci-Orellana, and Mohammed Abu-Nimer. 2005. *Faith-Based Peace-Building: Mapping and analysis of Christian, Muslim, and Multi-faith Actors*. The Hague: Netherlands Institute of International Relations.

Fitzgerald, Timothy. 2011. *Religion and Politics in International Relations. The Modern Myth*. London and New York: Continuum.

Gopin, Marc. 2000. *Between Eden and Armageddon: The Future of World Religions, Violence and Peacemaking*. New York and London: Oxford University Press.

Haynes, Jefffrey (ed.). 2023. *Routledge Handbook of Religion and Politics*, 3rd ed. London: Routledge.

Huntington, Samuel. 1996. *The Clash of Civilizations and the Remaking of World Order*. New York: Simon & Schuster.

Lasswell, Harold. D. 1936. *Politics: Who Gets What, When, How*. New York: Whittlesey House.

Marty, Martin, and Jonathan Moore. 2000. *Politics, Religion and the Common Good: Advancing a Distinctly American Conversation about Religion's Role in Our Shared Life*. San Francisco: Josey-Bass Publishers.

Moyser, George. 1991. 'Politics and religion in the modern world: an overview', in G. Moyser (ed.), *Politics and Religion in the Modern World*. London: Routledge, 1–27.

Norris, Pippa, and Ronald Inglehart. 2004. *Sacred and Secular. Religion and Politics Worldwide*. Cambridge: Cambridge University Press.

Ramet, Sabrina. 1995. 'Spheres of religio-political interaction: social order, nationalism, and gender relations', in Sabrina P. Ramet (ed.), *Render unto Caesar. The Religious Sphere in World Politics*. Lanham, MD: The American University Press, 51–70.

DOMESTIC POLITICS

STATE AND RELIGION

To comprehend the political importance of religion within countries, we need to look at its relationship with the state. When we refer to the *state*, we mean something more than the *government* alone. The state is the continuous administrative, legal, bureaucratic and coercive system that manages a country's political and administrative apparatus. As the political scientist, Alfred Stepan (1988: 1), noted many years ago: The state structures 'relations between civil and public power', as well as 'many crucial relationships within civil and political society'. All states necessarily engage with those representing significant religious faiths within their countries. They do this to control religion and to influence what it does politically. The Spanish sociologist of religion, José Casanova (1994) refers to this as the state's attempt to 'privatise' religion, that is, significantly to reduce religion's public influence.

> **INTRODUCTORY BOX: STATE AND CIVIL RELIGION IN THE USA**
>
> Like Iran, the USA is an example of a modernised country where politics and religion regularly interact with significant political effects. Unlike Iran, the USA is a country which long viewed religion as uniting rather than dividing citizens. This is the notion of *civil religion*. The state's aim is to create and consolidate a consensual,

> national religious expression, said to be guided by generalised, culturally appropriate, societally specific religious beliefs, not necessarily tied institutionally to any specific religious tradition (Haynes 2025). The state's strategy to champion civil religion aims to avoid serious social conflicts and promote national unity, necessary in a country which endured a damaging civil war in the 1860s. In recent years, the concept of civil religion has been undermined in the USA by the rise of significant polarisation, focused in what many see as the divisive politics of Donald J. Trump, US president between 2017 and 2021 (Haynes 2021).

As in the USA, relations between the state and religion in many countries have become more visible and increasingly problematic in recent years. This does not in itself constitute persuasive evidence against the idea that states in the contemporary era need or at least appreciate the kind of religious legitimation exemplified by civil religion. We certainly have to entertain the possibility that the recent proliferation of religion-based political challenges to the authority of the state are merely transitory reactions to continuing processes of secularisation, that is, the decreasing influence of religion in public life.

Interactions between the state and the leading religious organisation — if there is one — are often referred to as 'church-state' relations, even when the country in question does not have a leading Christian church. One of the difficulties in seeking to survey 'church'-state relations in the contemporary world is that the very concept of *church* derives from an Anglo-American viewpoint with relevance only to the Christian tradition. It is derived primarily from the context of what is called in England 'establishmentarianism' — that is, the maintenance of the principle of 'establishment' whereby one church is legally recognised as the established church. In England, that church is the Church of England whose Supreme Governor is the titular head of the Church, a position vested in the British monarch, in 2025, King Charles III.

When we think of 'church'-state relations we often assume a single relationship between two clearly distinct, unitary and solidly but separately institutionalised entities: state and church. Yet, both entities' jurisdictional boundaries need to be carefully delineated, to safeguard both separation and pluralism. This is because it is assumed that the leading church – like the state, which is the focal point of political power in a country – seeks institutionalised dominance over rival churches. The state, on the other hand, is compelled by law to respect individual rights even though it is assumed to be inherently disposed towards aggrandisement, that is, gaining ever more power, at the expense of citizens' personal liberty. In sum, the conventional concept of church-state relations is rooted in prevailing Western conceptions of the power of the state necessarily being constrained by forces in society – including religion – via what is known as *civil society*, which we examine below.

The traditional Western Christianity-derived perspective is that both state and leading church have a fair degree of power in relation to each other. Yet, when we look at the situation in, for example, Eastern Europe under communism in the decades after World War II until the 1990s when communist rule collapsed, there was a rather different situation. Communism was the dominant political system in more than 20 countries collected under the auspices of what was known as the Soviet Union, whose successor state is today's Russia. Under communist rule, the state presided over – and rigorously enforced – a monolithic unity with an institutional interpenetration of political-administrative and religio-ideological orders. In other words, the state dominated both politics and religion in the Soviet Union until the early 1990s when it collapsed.

BOX 2.1 THE STATE AND CHURCH IN FRANCE

Away from the Soviet Union, there were various European models of state-church relations. Everywhere in the region, a process of modernisation resulted in relatively powerful states which sought to control religion. In addition, the political importance of church-state issues declined as European states secularised and many Europeans became less religious.

We see a declining position for the church in relation to the power of the state over time. In France, the then-leading church, the Catholic Church, placed itself on the wrong side of the French

> Revolution in 1789, by strongly supporting the monarchy rather than the revolutionary forces. Following the revolution, the Catholic Church in France saw a precipitous decline in power, privilege and moral authority. Over time, the Catholic Church in France lost nearly all its influence.

Two points emerge from our brief survey of Europe's state-church relations:

- The state is more politically powerful than the church.
- The political importance of state-church issues declined over time.
- Widespread secularisation occurred in Europe, signifying a steady reduction in religion's influence on public affairs.

Turning to the global south, only in Latin America is it relevant to speak of church-state relations along the lines of the European/Christian model This is because of the historical regional dominance of the Roman Catholic Church and the creation of European-style states in the early nineteenth century following widespread imperial takeovers in Latin America by Spain and Portugal.

The traditional European-centric Christian conceptual framework of church-state relations appears alien within and with respect to nearly all African and Asian societies – whether predominantly Buddhist, Christian, Confucian, Hindu or Islamic. Expanding the concept of church-state relations to non-Christian contexts necessitates some preliminary conceptual clarifications – not least because the very idea of a prevailing state-church dichotomy is culture-bound. *Church* is a Christian institution, while the modern understanding of *state* is deeply rooted in the European political experience following what is known as the Reformation, when the dominance of the Roman Catholic Church was challenged by emerging 'Protestant' religious expressions. The Reformation lasted for more than a century (1517–1648) and was a widespread religious, cultural and social upheaval of the sixteenth century which ultimately led to the development of modern nation-states in Europe. It is widely acknowledged as one of the most important events in Western history.

In their specific cultural setting and social significance, the tension and the debate over the church-state relationship are uniquely Western phenomena, captured in the following biblical extract: 'render therefore unto Caesar the things which be Caesar's and unto God the things which be God's' (Luke 21: 25). This states that state and church have separate areas of focus and expertise and they should not meddle in each other's affairs. Overloaded with Western cultural history, these two concepts cannot simply be translated into non-Christian terminologies. Some religions – for example, Hinduism – lack a church – or, *ecclesiastical* – structure. As a consequence, there cannot logically be a Hindu institutional challenge to India's secular state comparable to that of, for example, Buddhist monks in South East Asia or Muslims learned in Islamic theology and sacred law in Iran, often referred to in the West as *mullahs*. In India, however, this has not stopped development of political parties and movements energised by notions of Hinduism's religious and social superiority. On such party, the Bharatiya Janata Party (BJP; 'Indian People's Party') is one of the two major Indian political parties alongside the Indian National Congress. Since 2014, the BJP has been the ruling political party in India under the incumbent Prime Minister Narendra Modi (Shani 2021).

Important differences between Christian conceptions of state and church and those of other world religions are well illustrated by reference to Islam. In the Muslim tradition, mosque is not church. The closest Islamic approximation to 'state' – *dawla* – means conceptually either a ruler's dynasty or administration. Only with the specific stipulation of *church* as the generic concept for *moral community*, *priest* for the *custodians of the sacred law*, and *state* for *political community* can we comfortably use these concepts in Islamic and other non-Christian contexts. Theologically, the 'command-obedience' relationship constituting the Islamic definition of authority is not demarcated by conceptual categories of religion and politics. This is because to many devout Muslims, life as a physical reality is an expression of divine will and authority (*qudrah'*). As a result, it is futile to attempt to separate matters of piety from those of the polity, because both are believed to be divinely ordained. On the other hand, while both religious and political authorities are seen to be Islamically legitimated, in modern Muslim-majority states, conceptually and often constitutionally, state and religion are independent institutions which regularly interact. The point is that in many contemporary Islamic interpretations polity and religion are not necessarily fused. On the other hand, there is a variety of different patterns to be found, with differing arrangements in current Islamic theocracies – Afghanistan, Iran, and Saudi Arabia – compared to countries where the state dominates religion, as in Algeria, Jordan, Malaysia and Turkey.

There is a variety of state-'church' relations. Table 2.1 presents some common arrangements.

A *theocracy* is a system of government where clerics rule in the name of God or a god. In a theocracy, religious authority is pre-eminent over secular power. A dominant religion seeks to shape the world according to leaders' interpretations of God's plan for humankind. Theocracies are rare in today's world. One of the most consistent effects of secularisation is to separate religious and secular power, often without regard for the religion or type of political system. However, events in various Muslim countries – Saudi Arabia after the country's creation in 1932, Iran after the 1979 Islamic revolution and Afghanistan in the 1990s and again from 2021 – indicate that theocracies can still happen even in today's increasingly secular world.

Table 2.1 Politics and religion: A comparative model

Theocracy	Generally religious	State churches	Liberal secular	Communist-secular
Afghanistan, Iran, Saudi Arabia	Indonesia, Spain, Poland USA	Denmark, England, Greece, Hungary, Malta, Zambia	France, Ghana. India, Netherlands, Turkey	China, Cuba, North Korea, Vietnam

BOX 2.2 IRAN'S 1979 THEOCRATIC REVOLUTION

Because of the pivotal role of Islam in the revolution, the 1979 overthrow of Iran's ruler – the Shah – was one of the most significant, yet unexpected, political events of recent times. Unlike earlier revolutions in Muslim-majority countries, such as in Egypt, Iraq, Syria and Libya, Iran's was not a secular, leftist revolution from above, but a massively popular overthrow of a widely derided monarch, the Shah. The outcome of the revolutionary process was a clerical, authoritarian regime. The Shah's regime was not a weak monarchy but a powerful centralised autocratic state with a strong and widely feared security service, the National Organisation for Intelligence and Security (*Sazeman-i Ettelaat va Amniyat-i* Keshvar, known as SAVAK) and a military, headed by an apparently loyal and cohesive officer corps.

Forces that overthrew the Shah came from all of Iran's urban social classes, nationalities, and ideologically different political parties and movements. An Islamic Republic was eventually declared. The *ulama* (Muslim clerics) organised in and by a new political party, the Islamic Republican Party, came to power. They established an Islamic constitution and proceeded to dominate the country's post-revolutionary political institutions until the present time.

The Iranian revolution was internationally significant. First, it was the first modern revolution characterised by religious ideology, forms of organisation, leading personnel and proclaimed goals. The Islamic holy book, the *Qur'an*, was the constitutional guide for Iran's post-revolution state, augmented by the *Sunnah* (i.e. the traditions of the Prophet Muhammad, comprising what he said, did, and of what he approved). Although economic and political factors played a major part in the growth of the anti-Shah movement, its religious leadership saw the revolution's goals primarily in terms of building an Islamic state which publicly rejected both capitalist materialism and liberal democracy.

From June 1989, radicals within Iran's ruling post-revolution elite began to lose ground following the death of Ayatollah Khomeini, the revolution's charismatic leader, which followed soon after the end of Iran's traumatic war with Iraq (1980–88). It was becoming clear that Iran's government was in need of foreign investment, technology and aid to help to secure the country's revolution. The lesson appeared to be that even a successful Islamic revolution

> could not succeed in splendid isolation. Iranians, like people everywhere, hope for improving living standards. It also became increasingly clear that many were not content with an Islamification of state and society, a process which for many Iranians was little more than a religious façade for extensive political and social repression.
>
> A self-proclaimed reformer, President Khatami, was elected to office in 1997 in a landslide victory but found himself caught between the demands, on the one hand, of those wanting social and political liberalisation and, on the other, the conservative *mullahs*. Khatami was unable to resolve the conundrum and a stalemate ensued between reformers and conservatives. Over the next decades, Iran's Islamic revolution faltered, with a series of both 'hardline' and 'reformist' presidents unable to take the revolution forward to the satisfaction of most ordinary people. In 2025, Iran is still controlled by a theocratic government but for many Iranians, the achievements of the 1979 revolution have been undermined by state repression and denial of opposition voices.

Second, some states are described as '*generally religious*', including the USA, Indonesia, Poland, and Spain. Such states are said to be guided 'generally' by religious principles, without being tied to a specific religious tradition. Belief in God is widely regarded as a key base on which the nation-state should develop. For example, in Indonesia, under the regime of General Suharto (1965–98), this belief was expressed in the concept of *Pancasila*.[1] In the USA, the notion of 'civil religion' reflects a similar concern with religious principles underlying the nation's development. Unlike *Pancasila*, the practice of civil religion in the USA is not formally recognised. Finally, there are several countries, including Spain and Poland, whose national principles include a prominent social role for the Roman Catholic Church.

Third, several countries have an *officially established faith*. Such countries, such as England, may also be rather secular. Even in many such countries, over time, established churches have often become of less public significance. In the case of the Anglican Church in England, for example, in the 1970s its public voice declined significantly before later regaining some significance in relation to societal demands for greater social justice under successive governments during a time of public 'austerity', a time when governments sought to reign in public spending.

The fourth model – *liberal secular* – is common in today's world. It captures the notion of secular power holding sway over religion, with clear distance, detachment and separation between church and state (Hallencreutz and Westerlund 1996: 2). The state strives to use religion for its own ends, to 'legitimate political rule and to sanctify economic oppression and the given system' of social stratification (Casanova 1994: 49). Secularisation is seen as a means of national integration in some post-colonial multi-religious states, such as Ghana and India, and no religion officially predominates. In aggressively modernising countries, such as post-Ottoman Turkey from the early 1920s, modernisation was expected to lead inevitably to a high and general level of secularisation; hence, successive constitutions in Turkey have been religiously neutral. This has not stopped religion from becoming involved politically in liberal secular states, including Ghana, India and Turkey. In these countries, democratisation and secularisation served to increasing religious involvement in politics. Ghana has recently seen the political rise of Christian nationalism, seen by its critics as a means to 'Christianise' politics in a constitutionally secular country. In India, the leading political party, the BJP, under the leadership of Narendra Modi, has championed the Hindu majority over the Muslim minority, which has led to persecution of the latter by the former, sanctioned by the government (Shani 2021). In Turkey, the Islam-orientated Welfare Party (*Refah Partisi*) achieved power via the ballot box in 1996. In 2002, its successor party, the Justice and Development Party (*Adalet ve Kalkınma Partisi*; AKP), achieved power. In 2025, the AKP still controlled the government and the state under the leadership of President Recep Tayyip Erdoğan. This indicates that even when secularisation is aggressively pursued over a long period as in Turkey, it does not necessarily imply that the political appeal of religiously orientated parties is doomed to disappear (Yavuz and Öztürk 2020).

Finally, there are *communist-secular states*. Communism is synonymous with a particular and dismissive attitude towards religion, sometimes described as 'anti-religion'. Some communist governments, such as that of Albania in the 1980s, decreed that religion was 'abolished'. In most communist regimes, however, religion was permitted and 'national religious organisations' existed. This arrangement was based on the understanding that religion was at most a private, spiritual concern of the individual only, strictly without expressed political interest or influence. This understanding constituted a promise that the communist state would respect people's religious faith and practice (as long as they did it behind closed doors as a solitary 'vice' not for public view). Communist states proactively use control of religion as a means to further the objective of total social control.

Paradoxically, however, even the most strident and prolonged state-communist anti-religion campaigns failed to secularise societies. When measured by the high levels of religiosity and the pivotal role of Christian churches in the turn to democracy in post-Soviet Central and Eastern Europe in the 1980s and 1990s, as well as the situation in non-communist but mostly secular-leaning Latin American countries and the revival of Islam in formerly communist Central Asia, it is clear that for many people living in such countries, religion retains immense significance.

Beyond the collapse of communist states in Central and Eastern Europe in the 1990s, there are still a few communist states in existence today, including the world's most populist state, China, as well as the Caribbean island of Cuba, North Korea and Vietnam. China controls the territory of Buddhist-majority Tibet, where the state enthusiastically seeks to teach atheism to Tibetan Buddhists so that Tibetans can, according to China's government, break free of the bewitchment of religion (https://freetibet.org/freedom-for-tibet/occupation-of-tibet/). In addition, China's communist state seeks to resuscitate Confucianism, an ancient Chinese religious tradition, as a means to try to inculcate what it sees as its desirable qualities during a time of unparalleled economic liberalisation.

POLITICAL SOCIETY

Today, there are various types of relationships between state and 'church' in countries around the world. None, however, is permanently able to resolve the tension between the secular world and religion. The chief manifestation of this tension in recent times is the desire of many religious organisations not to allow the state to sideline them as the state seeks to bite ever deeper into social life, a domain where religion once dominated. The result is that, around the world, many religious actors are today concerned with political and social issues. This leads to religion-based challenges to the status quo, which have their roots in state attempts to control religion. We can see this played out at three conceptually distinct levels: political society, civil society and the state itself.

The main stimulus for religion's politicisation, which dates from the mid-1970s, was a very significant political development known as the 'third wave of democratisation'. It began in 1974–75 with the overthrow of non-democratic regimes in three European countries: Portugal, Greece and Spain, before spreading to most parts of the world over the next quarter century. The third wave of democratisation eventually saw dozens of countries move from being ruled by governments not democratically chosen to new regimes whose leading personnel were chosen by voters in relatively free-and-fair elections (Huntington 1991). A widespread collapse of undemocratic governments was followed in many countries by attempts at democratisation, known as *democratic transitions*. Chances of democratisation are enhanced when there is (1) a strong civil society, (2) relative extensive amount of social capital and (3) a relatively unfragmented political society, with a stable party system.

What is known as *political society* is centrally involved at every stage of the process of democratisation. Democracy requires a great deal of planning and application, involving an array of political entities, including, leaders, parties, intra-party alliances, elections, electoral rules and legislatures. These entities comprise political society, which, while conceptually separate from civil society, is closely linked to it, especially during processes of democratisation.

The American political scientist, Alfred Stepan (1988: 3), explains that political society is the 'arena in which the polity specifically arranges itself for political contestation to gain control over public power and the state apparatus'. Political parties are one of the main components of political society. Chances of democracy taking root, the Italian political scientist, Giovanni Sartori (1991) argues, are bolstered when there are relatively few, not ideologically polarised, political parties competing for power. Autonomous, democratically organised, political parties can help to keep the personal power aspirations of political leaders in check. Another Italian political scientist, Leonardo Morlino (1998), argues that such political parties are a crucial key to democratic consolidation, that is, when democracy becomes habituated within a political system. Morlino also argues that the more rapidly a party spectrum forms during a democratic transition, then the more likely is eventual democratic consolidation. When party systems become institutionalised in this way, parties typically orient themselves towards the goal of winning elections through focused appeals to voters. On the other hand, when the political party structure is only slowly established, then citizens may respond better to personalistic appeals from populist leaders rather than to those of parties. This scenario tends to favour the former who may attempt to govern without bothering to establish and develop solid institutions underpinning their rule.

The main point is that institutionalising party systems matters a great deal as they are much more likely to help sustain democracy and to promote effective governance than the likely alternative: amorphous party systems dominated by populist leaders. An institutionalised party system can help engender confidence in the democratic process in four main ways. First, it can help moderate and channel societal demands into an institutionalised environment of conflict resolution. For example, in both India and Costa Rica, the party system helped over time to prevent 'landed upper class[es] from using the state to repress protests' (Rueschemeyer, Stephens and Stephens 1992: 281). Second, it can serve to lengthen the time horizons of actors because it provides electoral losers with the means periodically to mobilise resources for later rounds of political competition. Third, an effective party system can help prevent disenchanted groups' grievances from spilling over into mass street protests, likely to antagonise elites and their military allies and help facilitate a return to authoritarian rule ('the need for strong government'). Finally, an effective party system, linked to a capable state, can be important in helping imbue the mass of ordinary people with the idea that the political system is democratically accountable.

During democratisation, as with other organised interest groups, such as trade unions or ethnic minorities, religious leaders, organisations and activists, will feel free to critique the state of their country's politics. This is because, during democratisation, religion is freed from providing, often slavish, legitimacy to secular authority. Yet, if heightened concern about the state's policies is held up as evidence of the regeneration of the sociopolitical power of religion, one must still ask further questions. The issues are themselves secular and in so far as religious agencies are active in these areas, this is a radical shift of concern from the supernatural, from devotional acts, to what are largely secular goals to be pursued by secular means. However, a note of caution may be in order: We need to bear in mind that when religious actors function as pressure groups – rather than primarily as prayer bodies – they are not necessarily particularly effective. It is a rule of thumb that the more secular a society, the less likely it is that religion has a politically significant role.

During democratisation, we can see a range of religious responses which are in part dependent upon the degree of secularisation in a country. Religious responses include:

- resistance to the disestablishment and the differentiation of the religious from the secular sphere, that is, seeking to resist secularisation
- mobilisation and counter-mobilisation of religious groups and religiously-based political parties against other religions or against secular movements and parties
- religious groups' mobilisation in defence of religious, social and political freedoms

CIVIL SOCIETY

Civil society is the place where numerous social movements – including, neighbourhood associations, women's groups, religious groupings, intellectual currents and student associations – join with civic organisations – such as those mobilising lawyers, journalists, trade unions, and entrepreneurs – to constitute an ensemble of arrangements to express themselves and seek to advance their interests. The concept of *civil* society is sometimes used in contrast to *political* society. Unlike the latter, civil society refers to institutions and movements not involved in the business of government or in overt political management. This does not prevent civil society organisations from sometimes exercising profound political influence, on matters ranging from single issues to national constitutions.

Civil society is often important in transitions from authoritarian to democratic rule, in helping to select governments and monitor their performance when in office. Many examples of democratic transition during the third wave of democratisation reflected the importance of consistent political pressure on authoritarian regimes from 'below', that is, from civil society. Religious leaders and organisations are often important components of such civil society pressure (Edwards 2019). They help not only to extend the limits of newly created political space but are also instrumental in furthering democratisation through a transition phase, that is, when civil society's initial lead role is taken up by political society, typically via the formation of representative political parties. In many such cases, pressure leads non-democratic governments to liberalise, articulate political reform agendas and, eventually, allow relatively free and fair multiparty elections.

What is civil society? What are its origins? The term, 'civil society' crept quietly and largely unexamined into the political science literature in the 1980s, during the early stages of the third wave of democratisation. It began to be used in relation to the discourse of opposition leaders and groups in many non-democratic countries, especially in the then-communist countries of Central and Eastern Europe. Civil society is not however a new term. It is often associated with the German philosopher, Georg Wilhelm Friedrich Hegel (1770–1831), one of the most influential figures of German idealism and nineteenth-century philosophy. The term began to appear in the literature on Western political philosophy from the time of the emergence of the modern nation-state in the eighteenth century.

In contemporary usage, 'civil society' refers to associations and other organised bodies which are intermediate between the state and the family. These include, apart from religious organisations, labour unions, social movements, professional associations, student groups and the media. Collectively, as Stepan (1988) notes, such entities are thought crucial in maintaining a check on state power and its totalising tendencies; ideally, they amount to an ensemble of arrangements to advance the sociopolitical interests of society, with the state and civil society forming mutually effective counterweights. 'Strong' civil societies nearly always stem from strong societies. For the German political scientist, Thomas Risse-Kappen (1995: 22), ' "strong societies" are characterised by a comparative lack of ideological and class cleavages, by rather "politicized" civil societies which can be easily mobilized for political causes, and by centralized social organisations such as business, labor or churches'. In sum, 'civil society' is a key defender of society's interests against state (over-)dominance.

Civil society organisations are not directly involved in the business of government or overtly in political management of the state. But this does not necessarily prevent some from their exercising sometimes profound influence on various political issues, from single issues to the characteristics of national constitutions. For example, in Central and Eastern Europe from the 1980s, many observers identified the significant role of civil society in undermining hitherto strong communist regimes which uniformly toppled like dominoes during 1989–91. In short, the sudden and unexpected communist state system collapse in Central and Eastern Europe underlined the role that civil society could play in regime change.

There are three broad categories of civil society. First, there are *weak civil societies*, characteristic of societies fragmented by ethnic and/or religious divisions, and found in many African, Middle Eastern and Central Asian countries. In such examples, civil society is ineffective as a counterweight to state power. This is frequently linked to wider problems of governance, such as inadequate popular participation and lack of governmental transparency and accountability. In such circumstances, governments are typically adept at buying off or crushing expressions of discontent. Overall, these circumstances reflect failure or inability of social groups to organise so that they can defend and promote their interests, while seriously reducing societal capacity to counter the state's drive to gain ever more power.

Relatively strong civil societies are found in various East and South East Asian countries, including South Korea and Taiwan, and some Latin American and Central and Eastern European nations, including Argentina, Chile and the Czech Republic. *Strong civil societies* are found in most established democracies, for example, in India, Germany, Sweden and France. In both categories, civil societies are both vibrant and robust, with numerous civil rights organisations, social movements and local protest groups. One of the differences between 'strong' and 'relatively strong' civil societies is the length of time over which they have developed. Most Western European and North American countries have been states for lengthy periods, and their civil societies have also had a long time to develop, in some cases hundreds of years. On the other hand, Latin American and East Asian countries, while perhaps having been states for long periods, have nevertheless democratised much more recently. Countries with such civil societies are also normally nations not seriously divided by ethnic and/or religious schisms. They also tend to be relatively industrialised and urbanised, with well-organised trade unions and politically active working classes (Ogawa 2017).

When it comes to religion in civil society, we can note powerful civil religions – such as Evangelical Protestantism in nineteenth-century America – as well as the public intervention of religious pressure groups. The latter are typically concerned with single issues such as abortion or with a morally determined view of wider societal development. Trying to influence public policy – without however seeking to become political office-holders – religious leaders and organisations employ a variety of tactics, including (1) lobbying the state's executive apparatus, (2) going to court, (3) building links with political parties, (4) forming alliances with like-minded groups – whether secular or from other religions, (5) mobilising followers to protest and/or (6) seeking to sensitise public opinion through the mass and social media. The overall point is that religious actors may use a variety of methods to try to achieve their objectives.

In sum, in relation to the state, civil society's effectiveness is often linked to:

- societal – especially ethnic and religious – diversity, reflecting the quantity of social capital
- the level of economic development, urbanisation and industrialisation

SOCIAL CAPITAL

Civil society is most effective when it builds upon society's store of social connections, that is, its *social capital*. Whereas *human* capital comprises formal education and training, and *economic* capital is material and financial resources, *social* capital is the interpersonal trust that makes it easier for people to work collectively, neutralise free riders, and agree on what to do about non-performing governments.

The concept of social capital is widely employed in both political science and sociology, including in relation to political changes during the third wave of democratisation. Both civil society and political society are believed to be strengthened when there are 'sufficient' social connections in a society.

Social capital consists of relational ties and networks that can foster social norms, provide support and be leveraged for gain. Numerous studies indicate that social capital can positively influence educational achievement. The American political scientist, Robert Putnam, notes that religion is a leading source of social capital. However, there are relatively few studies examining variation in levels of social capital in various religious traditions, which leaves unanswered questions about the role of religion in shaping social capital (Park and Sharma 2016).

BOX 2.3   ROBERT PUTNAM ON SOCIAL CAPITAL

For the American political scientist specialising in comparative politics, Robert Putnam, social capital is of immense value in helping build and sustain democracy. Putnam argues that the level of trust in a society varies according to the vibrancy of associational life. In relation to Italy, Putnam tried to explain different institutional and economic performances of the country's regions as a consequence of the influence exerted by some aspects of the

> social structure, which he summarised into a multidimensional concept: 'social capital'. In short, for Putnam, the stock of social capital – which accrues from extensive and growing membership in voluntary associations – is likely to promote democratisation (Putnam 2000). Putnam's studies of the concept over the years have received much scholarly attention in a long-running debate in the social science literature, from both political scientists and economists.

A key advantage of the idea of social capital is that its widespread use facilitates an unprecedent level of cooperation and dialogue between scholars, policy makers and practitioners from different disciplines to work together, as they agree that the concept is both theoretically and practically useful. Portes and Zhou (1992) identify two main relational characteristics of social capital: First, what they call 'bonded solidarity', that is, the sense of common nationhood and cultural identity which helps focus group resources. Second, there is the 'enforceable trust' that controls the mutual assistance supplied and demanded, permitting a higher degree of resource sharing than would be conceivable through more informal channels. However, a society's 'bank' of social capital is likely to be undermined by:

- inefficient government performance
- authoritarian regimes that frown on the growth of societal solidarity
- widespread societal hardship
- social disintegration, due in part to development shortfalls

A key appeal of the concept is to be found in attempts to relate the functioning of a capitalist economy to a capitalist society's non-economic relations. Fine and Lapavitsas (2004: 17) find, however, that the concept is actually inadequate for this purpose – because, they argue, the notion of social capital contains confusion with regard to both capital as economic phenomenon and capitalist social relations. For them, the main problem is that 'social capital' conflates economy and society and hinders, rather than facilitates, analysis of capitalist society. This points to the fact that the concept of social capital is sometimes asked to do too much analytically. From the 1990s, the concept was introduced into almost every field of social science research. It was employed to try to explain an immense range of phenomena in the developing world, including political participation, institutional performance, success or failure of health care systems, degree of corruption in a society, public services' efficiency and a country's level of economic success.

While perspectives on social capital differ significantly in both origins and fields of application, they tend to agree on one key aspect: in relation to social structure, a relatively high level of social capital helps to generate positive results for group members, who thus acquire a competitive advantage in pursuing their ends. This is the case in many recent analyses of the developing world, where social capital has become popular not only in the design of development policies but also in what might be called the post-Washington Consensus policy agenda promoted not only by the World Bank and International Monetary Fund but also by various UN agencies. Failure of Washington Consensus policies in the developing world – seen as too top-down, too unresponsive to bottom-up demands – encouraged the view that both formal and informal social networks are *the* key resource underpinning people's successful achievement of collective actions. It encourages ability to participate in effective local decision-making, better monitoring of government agencies, improved ability to lobby for necessary collective services. Under circumstances where such attempts fail, social capital is a fallback, a resource that can help secure informal insurance from various sources, including friends, neighbours and the wider community. Failure of Washington consensus policies eventually led to a shift in World Bank thinking: local development projects were now often funded according to a perception of the strength of local voluntary organisations underpinning such funding applications. This was judged to be not only a vital way to promote more effective and better management of public services but also a more sensible way of pooling common community resources.

CONCLUSIONS

Religion's political impact of falls into two main – not necessarily mutually exclusive – categories. First, if the mass of people is not especially religious, as in the countries of Western Europe, then religious leaders and organisations often seek a public role as a result of their belief that society has taken a wrong turn. To redress this, what is needed, they claim, is a reintroduction of religious values to put society back on the straight and narrow. That is, religion will deprivatise, in order that its voice is heard in debates about a country's social and political direction. The aim is to be a significant factor in political deliberations so that religion's voice is consistently taken into account. To seek to accomplish this religious leaders seek popular support by addressing certain crucial issues, including not only the perceived decline in public and private morality but also the insecurities of life in an undependable market where for many greed and luck seem to be as effective as work and rational choice. In sum, religion's return to the public sphere is moulded by a range of factors, including the proportion of religious believers in society and the extent to which religious organisations perceive a decline in public standards of morality and compassion. Following the widespread disappointment at the outcomes of modernisation, religion seeks to focus and coordinate popular concern via political society and civil society, drawing on religious social capital to do so.

QUESTIONS

1. What is 'secularisation' and how does it affect the relationship between the state and religion?
2. Why did political science overlook religion for a long time?
3. How did the third wave of democratisation affect relations between religion and the state?
4. What are the main differences between political society and civil society?
5. What is social capital and how does it affect the political importance of civil society?

NOTE

1 The Pancasila idea is summed up in five principles: (1) *Kebangsaan* (nationalism), (2) *Kemanusiaan* (humanism or internationalism), (3) *Kerakyatan* (representative government or democracy), (4) *Keadilan Sosial* (social justice) and (5) *Ketuhanan* (monotheism).

FURTHER READINGS

Tsjeard Bouta, S. Ayse Kadayifci-Orellana, and Mohammed Abu-Nimer, *Faith-Based Peace-Building: Mapping and analysis of Christian, Muslim, and Multi-faith Actors*, The Hague: Netherlands Institute of International Relations, 2005. This is a useful introduction to interfaith dialogue covering three specific religions: Christianity, Judaism and Islam.

Timothy Byrnes, *Reverse Mission. Transnational Religious Communities and the Making of US Foreign Policy*, Washington, DC: Georgetown University Press, 2011. Byrne's book examines three US-based Christian networks that exert an important influence on US foreign policy involving communal not national loyalties.

Jeffrey Haynes, Peter Hough, and Bruce Pilbeam, *World Politics*, London: Sage, 2023. The authors provide a wide-ranging introduction to the field of international politics, useful as background and complementary reading to the present book.

Samuel Huntington, *The Clash of Civilizations*, New York: Simon and Schuster, 1996. Huntington's articulation of his controversial thesis – that the world is poised to enter an era of 'civilisational clashes' between Islam and Christianity – has been much debated, especially since 9/11.

Jack Snyder (ed.), *Religion and International Relations Theory*, New York: Columbia University Press, 2011. Snyder and his co-authors provide a definitive account of the current 'state of play' of how usefully to examine religion in international relations theory.

ONLINE RESOURCES

Pew Research Center. 'Religion & Politics. All Religion & Politics Publications'. www.pewresearch.org/topic/religion/religion-politics-1/

Religion, State and Society. Journal which publishes multidisciplinary research on the interplay of religion and political and social theory and practice, including political studies, sociology and more; some free access to relevant articles. www.tandfonline.com/journals/crss20

William Temple Foundation. 'Religion and Public Life: Top 15 Websites'. 'The internet can be an over-whelming place, so here at William Temple Foundation we're helping to streamline your surfing by gathering together a succinct collection of some of our favourite online resources devoted to various aspects of religion and public life. Below, we share our top 15 websites on religion and public life including places to find news, research, opinion pieces, and events.' https://williamtemplefoundation.org.uk/religion-and-public-life-top-15-websites/

REFERENCES

Casanova, José. 1994. *Public Religions in the Modern World*. Chicago and London: University of Chicago Press.

Edwards, Michael. 2019. *Civil Society*, 4th ed. Cambridge: Polity.

Fine, Ben, and C. Costas Lapavitsas. 2004. 'Social capital and capitalist economies', *South Eastern Europe Journal of Economics*, 1, 1: 17–34.

Hallencreutz, Carl F., and David Westerlund. 1996. 'Anti-secularist policies of religion', in Davd Westerlund (ed.), *Questioning the Secular State. The Worldwide Resurgence of Religion in Politics*. London: Hurst, 1–23.

Haynes, Jeffrey. 2021. *Trump and the Politics of Neo-Nationalism: The Christian Right and Secular Nationalism in America*. London: Routledge.

Haynes, Jeffrey (ed.). 2025. *Routledge Handbook of Politics and Religion in the Contemporary USA*. London: Routledge.

Huntington, Samuel. 1991. *The Third Wave. Democratization in the Late Twentieth Century*. Norman: University of Oklahoma Press.

Morlino, Leonardo. 1998. *Democracy between Consolidation and Crisis. Parties, Groups, and Citizens in Southern Europe*. New York: Oxford University Press.

Ogawa, Akihiro (ed.). 2017. *Routledge Handbook of Civil Society in Asia*. London: Routledge.

Park, Julie J., and Gitima Sharma. 2016. 'Religion and social capital: Examining the roles of religious affiliation and salience on parental network closure', *Religion and Education*, 43, 2: 162–77.

Portes, Alejandro, and Min Zhou. 1992. 'Gaining the upper hand: Economic mobility among immigrant and domestic minorities', *Ethnic and Racial Studies*, 15, 4: 491–522.

Putnam, Robert. 2000. *Bowling Alone. The Collapse and Revival of American Community*. New York: Simon and Schuster.

Risse-Kappen, Thomas. 1995. 'Bringing transnational relations back in: Introduction', in Thomas Risse-Kapen (ed.), *Bringing Transnational Relations Back In*. Cambridge: Cambridge University Press, 3–33.

Rueschemeyer, Dietrich, Evelyne Huber Stephens, and John D. Stephens. 1992. *Capitalist Development and Democracy*. Chicago: University of Chicago Press.

Sartori, Giovanni. 1991. 'Rethinking democracy: Bad policy and bad politics', *International Social Science Journal*, 29: 437–50.

Shani, Giorgio. 2021. 'Towards a Hindu *Rashtra*: *Hindutva*, religion, and nationalism in India', Religion, *State & Society*, 49, 3: 264–280.

Stepan, Alfred. 1988. *Rethinking Military Politics in Brazil and the Southern Cone*. Princeton: Princeton University Press.

Yavuz, M. Hakan, and Ahmet Erdi Öztürk. 2020. *Islam, Populism and Regime Change in Turkey*. London: Routledge.

INTERNATIONAL POLITICS

> **INTRODUCTORY BOX : INTERNATIONAL POLITICS AND RELIGION AFTER WORLD WAR II**
>
> After World War II, the number of countries grew considerably, increasing from fewer than 100 in 1945 to nearly 200 in 2025. This was due to several factors, notably decolonisation in the 1950s, 1960s and 1970s, and the collapse of the Soviet Union in the early 1990s. Among the world's nearly 200 countries, only three – Afghanistan, Iran and Saudi Arabia – are theocracies, that is, the state consistently refers to the country's majority religion (Islam in each of these three countries) as the state's guiding principle. No countries have Christian, Buddhist, Hindu or Jewish values and beliefs officially guiding state behaviour or policies.
>
> Many religious organisations and communities have not adapted to secular culture merely in order to survive – but instead have successfully developed their own identities and retained a focus on the supernatural in their beliefs and practices. Today, numerous religious actors are interested in and have an impact upon key areas of concern for international politics, including human rights – including, social justice, gender issues and democracy, human and economic development – and issues of conflict and cooperation: how to avoid the former and how to increase the latter.
>
> Around the world, numerous countries and regions provide evidence of continuing or growing interaction of religion and politics. These include the United States, with continued vitality of the

DOI: 10.4324/9781003508823-3

> Christian Right. The USA is an example of a constitutionally secular state which injects religion into its international politics, partly due to the influence of the Christian Right. The USA is a majority Christian country where three decades ago, 90% of US adults identified as *Christians*. In 2025, two-thirds of adults profess to be *Christians*. Recent US presidents, including George W. Bush (2001–2009), a 'born again' Christian, and Donald J. Trump (2017–21), had approaches to foreign policy, which were publicly influenced by their personal Christian beliefs. Bush claimed that it was God's will that the USA helped to spread religious freedom and democracy in the region, while Trump, politically beholden to the Christian Right, used his presidency to advance the cause of 'family values' at the United Nations and more generally in US foreign policy.
>
> Latin America's continuing Protestant evangelical surge significantly reduces the Roman Catholic Church's historical regional dominance, with social and political ramifications. In Central and Eastern Europe, the post-communist emphasis on religion significantly impacts on politics in many regional countries.
>
> In the Middle East and North Africa, there is a widespread Islamic renaissance, affecting political outcomes from Morocco to Egypt. In many sub-Saharan African countries, religion has a continuing high public profile, including in Nigeria, where it sometimes leads to political conflict. In addition, in India there is the persistent political significance of a Hindu nationalist political party, the Bharitiya Janata Party, and, finally, in Pacific Asia, several countries, including communist China and democratic South Korea, are experiencing a strong growth of Christianity.

Most countries officially organise both their domestic and international politics according to 'secular' principles – that is, where religious beliefs do not overtly inform or guide decision-making. The widespread absence of religious ideas or principles in international politics is the result of a basic principle, established in Europe over 375 years ago, following the 1648 Peace of Westphalia (comprising two international agreements signed in today's southern Germany). Over time, this principle spread throughout the rest of the world primarily by expansion of European influence – via imperialism, colonialism and trade expansion. The overall result is the widespread or downgrading of religious concerns, with secularity the dominant principle in international politics. As a consequence, once powerful religious leaders are publicly excluded from a formal role in international politics, just as they are from domestic politics in many countries.

The perceived superiority and desirability of secular power and authority over religion is both explicit and wide-ranging. It was the key ideological and organisational principle of two pivotal events in international politics, the American (1776) and French Revolutions (1789). Over time, European states collectively adopted the principle of the superiority of secular political power over that of religious authority. Spread to the rest of the world via European colonialism and imperialism in the eighteenth, nineteenth and early twentieth centuries, the outcome for international politics was that by the twentieth century, governments around the world pursued secular foreign policies.

BOX 3.1 THE STATE IN ISRAEL: RELIGION AND DEMOCRACY

Israel is often said to be a 'Jewish' country. This is because around 75% of Israel's population follow the Jewish religion. The state of Israel has been constitutionally secular since its founding in May 1948. This means that the state has secular democracy as its key guiding principle.

To state that Israel is secular is to note that since 1948 successive governments in Israel have claimed to adhere to secular not religious values, norms or principles in both domestic and foreign policy. On the other hand, governments in Israel do have significant 'religious' concerns. One in particular is very important, a consistent state goal, with both religious and security connotations. It is a state principle, one that extends to Israel's international politics and its relationships with neighbouring, Muslim-majority states, including Egypt, Jordan and Saudi Arabia, Israel's long-established policy is not to cede control of the Jewish holy city of Jerusalem to the mainly Muslim Palestinians. Muslims around the world regard Jerusalem as a holy city of Islam, the third most holy city in Islam after Mecca and Madinah.

Today, things are different and religion is an important component of international politics. This does not imply that people in most of the world's countries have decided that they should be run according to religious principles and ideas: 99% of the world's 200 countries apply secular principles to their international politics, most also apply them to their domestic politics.

The most significant category of religious actor[1] in international politics is not the state. It is the numerous *non-state religious actors*. Examples include the Roman Catholic Church, with its headquarters, the Vatican, in Rome; the Anglican (in America, Episcopal) Church, with its centre of operations in Canterbury, England; the World Council of Churches, a group of around 350 Protestant churches with its head office in Geneva, Switzerland; the Organisation of the Islamic Conference, a 57-member intergovernmental organisation of Muslim countries, whose headquarters is in Jeddah, Saudi Arabia; and a variety of transnational Islamist *jihadist* groups, often affiliated with long-established entities, including al Qaeda and Islamic State (Haynes 2021).

Until quite recently, religion was rarely mentioned in relation to international politics. We have already noted Iran's 1979 revolution, regarded by many countries, both in the West and the global south, as a major, religion-inspired, challenge to international stability and security. Three decades later, the al Qaeda attacks on the Twin Towers in New York and the Pentagon in Arlington, Virginia, on 11 September 2001 (widely referred to as '9/11'), reignited global concern about the destabilising impact of extremist Islam on international politics.

The threat of extremist Islam to destabilise international politics is only part of the story, albeit an important component. In addition, we are witnessing the outcome of a development which started with the end of the Cold War in the late 1980s and the subsequent collapse of the Soviet Union. To understand why we are today concerned about religion in international politics, when a few years ago we were not, we need to refer both to a specific event ('9/11') and to longer term developments linked to the demise of the Soviet Union.

On 9/11, three aeroplanes on domestic flights in the USA were hijacked by Islamic terrorists. Most hijackers were nationals of either Saudi Arabia or Egypt. Yet their main allegiance was not to a country or a government; instead, it was to Osama bin Laden and a transnational Islamist terrorist organisation, al Qaeda. On 9/11, al Qaeda operatives compelled the aeroplanes' pilots to divert their flight paths and to turn them into weapons of mass destruction. Two of the planes hit their intended targets – the Twin Towers of the World Trade Centre in New York and the Pentagon in Virginia – with the collective loss of nearly 3,000 lives. The al Qaeda personnel regarded their selected targets as highly symbolic of American capitalist (Twin Towers) and military (the Pentagon) power. The outcome of the attacks was that for international politics, 12 September 2001, was a very different day compared to September 10. Suddenly, religion was centrally on the international politics agenda. Overnight, the world dramatically changed.

What was the impact of 9/11 on international politics? Was 9/11 the first shot in an escalating conflict between America and extremist Islamists? Or was it the last gasp in a clash which actually began many years earlier, in 1978? This was the year the Soviet Union (also referred to in English as the Union of Soviet Socialist Republics [USSR], the precursor to today's Russia) invaded Muslim-majority Afghanistan. The USSR's aim was to keep Afghanistan's communist president in power following an insurgency by local Islamists. This failed and the Soviet Union's defeat in Afghanistan was one of the factors that led to its sudden collapse a dozen years later.

The USSR's disintegration also marked the end of the Cold War, a four decades long conflict between the United States and the Soviet Union, which started soon after World War II ended in 1945. The Cold War centred on a battle for supremacy between competing secular ideologies: liberal democracy/capitalism (USA) and 'Godless' communism (Soviet Union). Religious rivalry was not an important factor in the Cold War.

The importance of the Cold War was so great for international politics that most analysts were not that concerned with anything else for more than 40 years after World War II until the Cold War ended. Then, suddenly, the pre-existing international system changed dramatically. The 'bipolar' – that is, two poles, the USA and the USSR – system was abruptly replaced by a fragmented 'multipolar' – that is, 'many poles' – power structure, featuring several significant countries, including Brazil, China, France, Germany, India, Nigeria, the United Kingdom and the United States of America.

The key point is that the quarter century between the USSR's invasion of Afghanistan in 1978 and the events of 11 September 2001, was a period of fundamental change for international politics. In addition to these two, we can add a third factor of major – and continuing – importance for understanding religion's significant role in today's international politics: globalisation (Haynes, Hough and Pilbeam 2023).

GLOBALISATION AND RELIGION

A continuing technological revolution is a key component of contemporary globalisation, including a massive growth in the spread of the internet and electronic communications. The implication of this for our purposes is that numerous non-state religious actors now easily organise activities across state borders, that is, they form effective and purposive transnational networks. Apart from solely religious goals, transnational religious actors pursue a range of secular objectives, including cooperation, conflict, development, democratisation, security, and human rights.

How does globalisation affect the relationship between religion and politics? Do religious actors have a capacity to undermine state sovereignty, that is, to 'talk' directly to religious believers across international boundaries beyond state control? To answer these important questions, we start by looking at the impact of historic globalisation on the relationship between state and religion.

Some observers contend that there is a global resurgence of religion which must be seen in a historical context. We have noted that, over time, religion lost most of its earlier political significance during the development of modern states. Prior to that, that is, before the seventeenth century, both Islam and Christianity were global political actors. Islam expanded from its Arabian heartland in westerly, easterly, southerly and northern directions for nearly a millennium from the seventh century. As a result, vast territories in Africa and Asia and smaller areas of Europe (parts of the

Balkans and much of the Iberian Peninsula) came under prolonged Muslim control. Unable to deal with the consequences of centralised Christian polities in Western Europe – especially, superior firepower and organisational skills – Islam found itself on the back foot. The consequence was a significant reduction in Islam's influence in Europe from the late fifteenth century. However, despite this significant setback, Islam developed into a holistic religious, social and cultural system in many parts of the world, becoming a world religion via transnational religious communities.

Christendom is another historic example of a transnational religious society that developed under historical conditions of globalisation. During medieval times 'Christendom' referred to a generalised conception among Christians of being subject to universal norms and laws derived from the word of God. Later, and contemporaneous with the demise of Islam as a major force in Europe, the expansion of Europeans to non-European areas facilitated the growth of transnational Christian communities, divided by differing interpretations of Christianity, that is, Roman Catholic and Protestant.

BOX 3.2 CHRISTIANITY AND COLONIALISM

The transnational spread of Christianity beyond Europe was facilitated by colonisation, which began in the late fifteenth century with a search for gold in the Americas by sundry Spanish and Portuguese 'explorers'. This led, soon after, to the establishment in the 'New World' of various Spanish or Portuguese-administered colonies; contemporaneously, different Christian Europeans – British, French and Dutch – gained territory in the Caribbean and in parts of Asia. Thus, the spread of Christianity was inextricably linked to wider European expansionism, to become a major component of an emerging web of global interactions. Over time, however, the public and political role of Christianity became increasingly marginal, following the rise to prominence of secular states in Europe and elsewhere. After the Treaty of Westphalia in 1648 (which ended the religious wars in Europe between Catholics and Protestants), the history of the development of the global state system was primarily the history of clashing secular nationalisms, with each national group aiming for its own state and with a significantly reduced political role for religion.

Both Christian and Muslim transnational religious communities predated the emergence of centralised secular states. Prior to the seventeenth century, religious interactions were pivotal to the development of a system of international politics and economics. Christianity and Islam grew to become world religions, conveying their associated civilisations around the world via colonisation, conquest and the expansion of global trade. Contending religious beliefs were the chief motor of international conflicts, the main threat to peace and security. However, the political importance of religion in international politics became increasingly insignificant from the seventeenth century, re-emerging as politically important only in the late twentieth century, encouraged by globalisation and the accompanying communications revolution.

The last two decades of the twentieth century was an era of fundamental global political, social and economic changes, associated with the multifaceted processes commonly referred to as 'globalisation'. Globalisation not only emphasised consolidation of a global economy and, to some, the gradual emergence of a 'global culture', but was also manifested in other various political and social developments, notably the third wave of democracy and increased focus on human rights. Finally, as already noted, many countries saw increased political involvement of religion.

BOX 3.3 GEORGE WEIGEL AND 'UNSECULARIZATION OF THE WORLD'

Increased political involvement of religion in recent decades stimulated the American Catholic neoconservative author, political analyst, and social activist, George Weigel, to claim there is a global religious revitalisation, or, as he put it: an 'unsecularization of the world' (quoted in Huntington 1993: 26).

Weigel did not mean to imply that this was 'only' an *apolitical* respiritualisation. He also pointed to a more general reengagement of religion and politics, facilitated by globalisation and encouraged by the communications revolution. The consequence, as Beyer (2003: 333) notes, is that we live in 'a globalizing social reality, one in which previously effective barriers to communication no longer

> exist'. The development of transnational religious communities was greatly enhanced by ease of interpersonal and intergroup communications, facilitating the spread of their messages and enabling such groups to form regional or global networks. If Wiegel is right and there is an 'unsecularization of the world' with political connotations, we should be able to pinpoint examples of such a process linked to the transnational spread of religion.

The American sociologists, Robert Wuthnow and Stephen Offut (2008) define globalisation 'as the increasing flow of people, information, goods, services, and other resources across national boundaries'. Globalisation is significantly altering social contexts in ways that influence religious practices. Today, religion is not only reflected in local communities and national societies but is also linked with networks that span societal borders. While immigration is the most studied example, other flows of people and resources also need to be considered, as do the transnational political and economic influences that shape religion.

BOX 3.4 TRANSNATIONALISM AND RELIGION

Theoretical literature on transnationalism devotes relatively little concentrated attention to religious phenomena. This is because transnational linkages and penetration are typically studied in the international politics literature primarily to assess their impact on questions of political and economic security. The conventional security bias of much of the transnational literature helps explain the lack of references to religious actors (Haynes 2021). Until the emergence of transnational Islamist actors in the 1980s, religious actors were usually regarded as an interesting phenomenon, although remote from the central questions affecting states and state power in international politics. The explanation for this relative neglect lies in a key assumption embedded in the social sciences. One presupposition, especially evident in theories of modernisation and political development, was that the future of the integrated nation-state lay in secular participatory politics. The implication was that, in order successfully to build nation-states,

> political leaders would have to remain as neutral as possible from the entanglements of particularist claims, including those derived from religion. The connotation was that politics must be separated from religion (and ethnicity) so as to avoid dogmatism and encourage tolerance among their citizens. As decades of apparently unstoppable movement towards increasingly secular societies in the Western and other 'modernised' parts of the world suggested, over time religion and piety became ever more private matters. The consequence was that religion was relegated to the category of a problem that must not be allowed to intrude on the search for national unity and political stability.

How to explain the widespread involvement of religious actors in international politics? We saw in Chapter 2 that religious actors directly affect the internal politics of states and thus qualify state power, as conventionally understood. Globalisation is significant in this context for two main reasons. First, globalisation facilitates the transmission of both material and nonmaterial factors, and religious actors may seek to use opportunities to spread messages, funds and personnel. Second, our case studies show that the domestic impact of religion is always contoured by particular social and political circumstances in individual countries.

INTERNATIONAL POLITICS AND RELIGION

What does increased involvement of religion in international politics imply for our understanding of these two phenomena? In this regard, the American political scientist, Jack Snyder (2011), poses two useful questions:

- What is distinctive about religious subject matter in international politics?
- What are the 'implications for the kinds of theories and methods that are needed to study' religion in international politics?

For Snyder (2011), 'religion is one of the basic forces of the social universe, not just an "omitted variable"'. A pair of American international politics analysts, Daniel Philpott and Timothy Samuel Shah (2011), point out that 'religion is older than the state, and its aims encompass not just politics but all of life'. A third American, Chris Seiple (2011: 292), an international relations analyst, claims that as religion 'pre-dates the field of international' politics it 'has been and will always be integral to human identity'. These comments underline that for these four American scholars, religion is of such great importance in today's world that it is inevitable that it will be of importance to analyses of international politics. As religion is a universal phenomenon, it has both social and political importance for billions of people around the world. These include key political decision-makers, including presidents, prime ministers, foreign ministers and so on. But the preferences of individual decision-makers are not the only factor we need to take into account when thinking of religion in international politics. The importance of religion in international politics today is manifested further in three ways. First, religions go beyond state borders – that is, they are very often cross-border or, in international politics terminology, they are 'transnational actors'. Second, because of wide-ranging concerns, religion affects many of society's institutions, norms and values – that is, religion often impacts how actors in international politics behave. Third, religions may strongly inspire believers to act in certain ways and not others – that is, religion can be a stimulus to action both for individuals and groups involved in international politics.

But to understand today's return of religion to international politics, we need to locate current events in a historical context. We have already seen secular international politics is conventionally dated from the Peace of Westphalia. This was an international treaty signed in what is today Germany in 1648. Germany, like Christendom generally, saw its religious map fundamentally redrawn following Christianity's Protestant Reformation. This led to the end of the previous dominance of the Roman Catholic Church. Beyond religion, the Reformation was a tumultuous upheaval which greatly affected Western Europe, politically, economically and socially. As already noted, formerly dominant religious ideas were largely replaced by new secular ideologies over the next century, manifested in the revolutions in America (1776) and France (1789). Both stressed the importance of representation, legitimacy and popular authority.

One reason why these historical precedents are very important when seeking to analyse the role of religion in international politics today, is that, as Snyder remarks, they raise 'the possibility that comparable new [religious] upheavals could once again produce far-reaching changes in the international system' (Snyder 2011). Snyder is thinking in particular of the impact of 9/11 on international relations. A few years before 9/11, an American academic, Samuel Huntington (1996), controversially argued that in the post-Cold War world, international relations was becoming characterised by what he called a 'clash of civilisations'. The 'clash of civilisations' referred to what Huntington saw as an emerging conflict between 'Islam' – that is, the large bloc of 'Muslim' countries – and the 'West', that is, western European and North American states.

Huntington turned out to be wrong, as no such clash ensued. Yet the continuing impact of his thesis had an important effect upon how many people, including scholars and policy makers, understand and view international politics. We can understand increased involvement of the USA and other Western countries, including the United Kingdom, in the Middle East in the decade since 9/11 as being directly linked to Huntington's view of the world, reflected in recent and current Western involvement in Afghanistan, Iraq, and Libya. In each case, the main concern is to deter extremist Islamists and encourage 'moderate' Muslims.

To answer Snyder's first question – What is distinctive about religious subject matter in international' politics? – we can respond that it is distinctive in the sense that it brings into international politics the issue of norms, values and beliefs that go beyond the traditional secular concerns of international politics, that is, war, peace and security. This opens up the terrain of international politics analysis to the involvement of numerous non-state actors motivated by religious concerns. In response to Snyder's second question: What are the 'implications for the kinds of theories and methods that are needed to study' religion in international politics? It is a necessary factor in religious involvement when it is there and not to discount it from our theories and methods because we believe that the universe of international politics is best explained by secular theories alone.

How might religion be brought into, and augment and illustrate, existing concepts, theories or paradigms of international politics? Do we need new ones as a result of the wide-ranging concerns of religion's recent and current involvement and international politics? The Israeli political scientist, Jonathan Fox and the Turkish political scientist, Nukhet Sandal, suggest we should work within mainstream international politics theoretical paradigms of realism, liberalism and constructivism to assess the influence of religion in shaping outcomes in international politics. They contend that this helps in defining and explaining the actions of associated key actors – both states/governments and non-state actors. Fox and Sandal (2013) try to accommodate the multiple ways in which religion and world affairs interact by adapting international politics to include religion's various impacts. Their approach is to develop a comprehensive list of ways in which religion can potentially influence international politics, then to take this list and examine whether and how each item can be explained by use of traditional – that is, secular – theories of international politics. Critics, such as the Austrian political scientist, Jodok Troy, contend that the outcome is that their approach is 'inevitably reductive', providing 'sometimes idiosyncratic readings and interpretations of the already existing theoretical framework ... for example, Realism' (Troy, 2015).

POST-SECULAR INTERNATIONAL POLITICS

The term, post-secular, is now widely used in various academic disciplines, including not only political science, international politics and political philosophy but also in sociology, theology and history. For sociologists, the 'post-secular' is in the context of a (generally) unexpected return of religion into previously secularised societies. In this view, the post-secular is characterised by new visibility of religious practices and religious attitudes in previously secular public spaces, including those in Western Europe, previously believed to be inexorably secularising.

BOX 3.5   JÜRGEN HABERMAS ON 'POST-SECULAR' EUROPE

There have been various attempts to conceptualise the post-secular in international politics, notably in the work of the German sociologist and philosopher, Jürgen Habermas (2006). Habermas states that he is trying to answer the question of why we can now term some 'secularised' societies in Europe as 'post-secular'. In such societies, including for example, the United Kingdom, Germany and the Netherlands, various religious actors seek greater public influence, relevance and significance. This comes in the context of earlier secular certainty losing explanatory power for what is happening in Europe, with the continuing general impact of globalisation and that of the post-2008 economic crisis. Habermas points out that at some stage what is now a 'post-secular' society must at some point have been located in a 'secular' country. Logically, then, the controversial term – post-secular – can only be applied to the apparently secular societies of Europe, as well as Western countries including Canada, Australia and New Zealand. In each, popular religious ties have steadily lapsed, often dramatically in recent decades. These countries and regions show pretty conclusively that citizens live in a secularised society. Habermas notes that in terms of sociological indicators in such places, there is no widespread return to religious behaviour and associated convictions among local populations. Trends towards de-institutionalised and new spiritual forms of religiosity have not offset the tangible losses by the major religious communities. According to Habermas, three overlapping phenomena converge to create the impression of a widespread 'resurgence of religion': an expansion in missionary activities, a 'fundamentalist' radicalisation and a political instrumentalisation of the potential for violence innate in many of the world's religions.

For political scientists, evidence of post-secularity is to be found in the necessity of re-evaluating how governments engage with religion and adapting their policies to requirements of increasingly religiously pluralist societies in, for example, Western Europe, long regarded as moving inexorably along the path of secularisation. In addition, there is the issue of religious freedom and the role of religious actors in the public sphere in Western Europe's increasingly multicultural national environments.

Political philosophers view 'post-secularity' as a normative challenge that, on the one hand, defines the place of religious viewpoints in the democratic public sphere and, on the other, serves to formulate a political ethic with general validity among citizens, irrespective of which faith – if any – they belong to. Philosophers address questions about the relevance of religiously informed arguments in morality and ethics debates, including those to do with gender equality, women's right and access to abortion services, and the scourge of HIV/AIDS and how to deal with the pandemic.

Theologians often examine 'post-secularity' as a condition within which Christian churches and other institutionalised religious identities strive to find both place and role in relation to the state and civil society, which are no solely longer determined – at least in Western Europe – by exclusively secularist criteria. Finally, historians place 'post-secularity' in the broader historical context of modernisation and cultural history, aiming to identify specific historical processes and conditions that led to secularisation and now, perhaps, lead out of it.

What might a post-secular international politics look like? Is there persuasive evidence that international politics is today characterised to a significant extent by a 'renewed openness to questions of the spirit' leading to a 'renewed interest in the spiritual life'? Among other factors, declining membership of organised religions and growth of secularism, especially in the West, have led to a broader view of spirituality. 'Spiritual' today is often used in contexts where 'religion' would once have been the preferred term in which the term 'religious' was formally employed. While the term 'post-secular' is used in a variety of ways, most meanings point to complex and diverse changes that in different ways involve a resacralisation[2] or revitalisation of religion. However, this new situation provides researchers with not only a theoretical challenge but also a methodological one for understanding the impact on international politics. For example, as a result of the changes that may be occurring, it becomes difficult to focus only on religious groups, organisations or movements; as many and varied forms of post-secular religious phenomena now exist, for example, spiritual practices that are not associated with any religious faith or tradition. Traditionally, theorists of international politics sought to reduce the study of religion in international politics to a small number of discrete actors: religious organisations of various kinds, including interest groups with moral and/or ethical concerns at one end of the spectrum to extremist and terrorist entities at the other end.

CONCLUSION

This chapter is concerned with how religion can usefully be brought into concepts, theories or paradigms of international politics. We saw that some scholars – such as Samuel Huntington– believe that a new theory of international politics is necessary to explain this. Fox and Sandal (2013), on the other hand, contend that it is possible to accommodate the multiple ways in which religion and international politics interact by adapting existing IR theories to incorporate religion's influence. Finally, there are those, such as the Turkish political scientist, Ahmed Erdi Öztürk (2021), who argues that religion's influence is most significant in specific ways and in specific contexts related to religion's power in relation to other aspects of international politics.

Overall, the chapter sought briefly to survey current scholarly approaches to the study of religion and international politics. The chapter pointed out that since the late 1970s, kick-started by the Islamic Revolution in Iran, the topic emerged. As it developed, it was identified/identifiable as a discrete area of study, separated into two chronological periods: pre-11 September 2001 ('9/11') (late 1970s–11 September 2001) and post-9/11 (post-11 September 2001). The first period was consequential to Iran's Islamic revolution, and in addition Huntington presented his influential 'clash of civilisations' paradigm. The second period, post-11 September 2001, saw a growing number of scholarly accounts focusing on religion in international politics. Many regarded 9/11 as pivotal, highly influential in helping remake Western foreign policies, as over the next decades Western governments appeared fixated on Islamist extremism and terrorism. Over time, however, characterised by the apparently significant diminution of the threat to the West of Islamist terrorism following the apparent demise of the Islamic State and the fragmentation and reduction in influence of al Qaeda, new foci appeared in relation to religion's influence in international politics.

To conclude this chapter, we pose a couple of question: When it comes to the association of religion and international politics, what do we know and how do we know it? To what extent do we need to change our perception of religion's (relatively minor but not marginal) impact on international politics in order to make better theory? It seems clear that there is no succinct answer to these questions. In response to the first – What do we know? – we observed that empirical events help explain the rise and fall of concern with the role of religion in international politics, and that theoretical innovation needs to take 'real world' events into account to make better theory. In response to the second question – 'How do we know it' – we engaged with evidence that scholars focus on what they think is most important and that there are various methodological and theoretical ways to find out more about the issue that they examine. In short, there is no single way to make theoretical progress in explaining and understanding the role(s) of religion in international politics theories.

We conclude by emphasising that we live in a hierarchical and multipolar, but also interdependent and multilateral, global system, which significantly developed after the Cold War. For international politics theory, religion is not a 'game changer', although its various manifestations – expressed in the actions and reactions of both states and transnational non-state actors – can at times and in relation to certain issues be significant. However, religion's 'return' to international politics does not imply that we must fundamentally adjust our understanding of how international politics 'works' or how it is theorised. The long-running focus on the activities of states – which still in the main adhere to secular principles and objectives in their foreign policies and international politics – is still to be captured within existing international politics theories which collectively see little consistent significance for religion. Religion remains an intriguing, yet often opaque, component of how we understand international politics.

QUESTIONS

1. What are the indications that religion is an important factor in international politics?
2. What do you understand by the term 'post-secular'?
3. Have we entered a new era of post-secular international politics? If so, what is the evidence that this shift has occurred?
4. To what extent does globalisation encourage the growth and spread of religious transnational actors?
5. How would you theorise the involvement of religion in international politics today?

NOTES

1 Toft, Philpott and Shah (2011: 23) define a religious actor as 'any individual, group, or organization that espouses religious beliefs and that articulates a reasonably consistent and coherent message about the relationship of religion to politics'. A religious actor is encouraged to undertake action by religious faith. Such actors include churches and comparable religious organisations in non-Christian religions; religious social movements, whose main motivating factor is their members' religious beliefs; and political parties, whose ideology has roots in identifiable religious beliefs and traditions.
2 Resacralisation refers to the return of religious meanings to the public realm, including in relation to politics, the arts and resistance to secularisation, especially from religious believers.

FURTHER READING

Peter Berger (ed.), *The Desecularization of the World. Resurgent Religion and World Politics*, Washington, DC: Ethics and Public Policy Center, 1999. This volume challenges the belief that the world is increasingly secular, showing that while modernisation does have secularising effects, it also provokes a reaction that more often strengthens religion.

Jürgen Habermas, 'Religion in the public sphere', *European Journal of Philosophy*, 14, 1, 2006, pp. 1–25. This article is widely cited in relation to the notion of the postsecular in international politics. It focuses upon the most secular of regions – Europe – and seeks to assess the extent to which it can now be understood as postsecular.

Jeffrey Haynes, *Religious Transnational Relations and Soft Power*, Aldershot: Ashgate, 2012. The aim of this book is to examine selected religious transnational actors in international politics, with a focus on both security and order.

Jeffrey Haynes (ed.), *Handbook on Religion and International Relations*. London: Edward Elgar, 2021. This comprehensive handbook examines the relationship between religion and international politics, mainly focusing on several world religions – Christianity, Islam, Hinduism and Judaism. Providing a timely update on this understudied topic, it evaluates how this complex relationship has evolved over the last four decades, looking at a variety of political contexts, regions and countries.

Pippa Norris and Ronald Ingelhart, *Sacred and Secular. Religion and Politics Worldwide*, Cambridge: Cambridge University Press, 2004. This book develops a theory of secularisation and existential security and compares it against survey evidence from almost 80 societies worldwide.

ONLINE RESOURCES

E-International Relations. 'Religion and Culture in International Relations'. 'A collection of multimedia and textual resources that help unpack, and explain, the importance of religion and culture and how they intersect.' www.e-ir.info/2022/03/28/religion-and-culture-in-international-relations/

Elgar Online. *Handbook on Religion and International Relations*. Elgar Handbooks in Political Science. www.elgaronline.com/edcollbook/edcoll/9781839100239/9781839100239.xml

The Review of Faith & International Affairs. 'An international journal publishing innovative research and policy-relevant analysis on the role of religion in global affairs and public life worldwide.' www.tandfonline.com/journals/rfia20

REFERENCES

Beyer, Peter. 2003. 'Constitutional privilege and constituting pluralism: Religious freedom in national, global, and legal context', *Journal for the Scientific Study of Religion,* 42, 3: 333–9.

Fox, Jonathan and Nukhet Sandal. 2013. *Religion in International Relations Theory: Interactions and Possibilities*. London and New York: Routledge.

Habermas, Jürgen. 2006. 'Religion in the public sphere', *European Journal of Philosophy*, 14, 1: 1–25.

Haynes, Jeffrey. 2021. 'Religion, nationalism, and transnational actors'. In *The Oxford Research Encyclopedia of International Studies*. Oxford University Press. Details at https://oxfordre.com/internationalstudies/display/10.1093/acrefore/9780190846626.001.0001/acrefore-9780190846626-e-417

Haynes, Jeffrey, Peter Hough, and Bruce Pilbeam. 2023. *World Politics*. London: Sage.

Huntington, Samuel. 1993. 'The clash of civilisations?', *Foreign Affairs*, 72, 3: 22–49.

Huntington, Samuel. 1996. *The Clash of Civilizations*. New York: Simon and Schuster.

Öztürk, Ahmet Erdi. 2021. *Religion, Identity and Power: Turkey and the Balkans in the Twenty-First Century*. Edinburgh: Edinburgh University Press.

Seiple, Chris. 2011. 'From ideology to identity: Building a foundation for communities of the willing', in Patrick James (ed.), *Religion, Identity, and Global Governance. Ideas, Evidence, and Practice*. Toronto: University of Toronto Press, 292–310.

Snyder, Jack (ed.). 2011. *Religion and International Relations Theory*. New York: Columbia University Press.

Toft, Monica Duffy, Daniel Philpott, and Timothy Samuel Shah. 2011. *God's Century. Resurgent Religion and Global Politics*. New York and London: W.W. Norton and Company.

Troy, Jodok. 2015. 'Little Do They Know. How (Not) to Theorise Religion and International Relations'. *E-International Relations*. www.e-ir.info/2015/09/11/little-do-they-know-how-not-to-theorise-religion-and-international-relations/

Wuthnow, Robert, and Stephen Offut. 2008. 'Transnational religious connections', *Sociology of Religion*, 69, 2: 209–32.

CONTENTIOUS POLITICS

INTRODUCTORY BOX : WHAT ARE CONTENTIOUS POLITICS?

American sociologist and political scientist, Charles Tilly (2015), defines contentious politics as 'interactions in which actors make claims bearing on someone else's interest, in which governments appear either as targets, initiators of claims, or third parties'. In order to make a political point or to try to change government policy, contentious politics involves the use of disruptive techniques, which distinguishes from 'normal' politics. Disruptive techniques in this context include demonstrations, strike actions, direct action, riot, terrorism, civil disobedience, insurrection, rebellion and revolution.

The concept distinguishes these forms of contention from what the political scientist, James C. Scott (1985), calls 'everyday acts of resistance', that is, forms of contention employed entirely within institutional settings, such as elections.

While contentious politics has always existed, Tilly (2015) explains that the nature of contentious politics changed significantly in eighteenth-century Europe with the birth of social movements. Over time, the concept of contentious politics developed, and much work has been done on the topic by significant scholars, including not only Tilly but also by fellow Americans, such as Sidney Tarrow and Doug McAdam.

DOI: 10.4324/9781003508823-4

CONTENTIOUS POLITICS AND RELIGION

We saw in earlier chapters that relationships between religion and politics help to mould people's attitudes about the way that political systems, both domestically and internationally, are organised and operate. Sometimes these relationships are expressed in relation to contentious politics.

Conceptually separate, religion and politics are often intertwined, and relationships between them evolve over time. This chapter examines the issue of religion in relation to contentious politics, linked to areas of significant political and social contestation. We look at four issues in some detail in the chapter for two reasons, first, religious involvement is pronounced, and, second, religions have been used in various ways to try to get the outcomes that activists wish to see:

- democratisation and democracy
- right-wing populism
- culture wars
- religious terrorism

Religious involvement in contentious politics developed over time. The initial research field of religious involvement in politics emerged in the decades after World War II, focused somewhat narrowly on the relationship between Christianity and the development of modern states in Europe. Over time, owing to the impact of decolonisation in the 1960s, the end of the Cold War in the late 1980s and the continuing impact of globalisation, the subject matter of religion and contentious politics expanded both in terms of geographic extensiveness – to cover much of the globe – and in relation to the number of religious faiths included in the research focus.

Following decolonisation in the global south from the late 1940s, Western-derived politics and ideologies influenced the political development of much of the non-Western world, including Africa, Asia, Latin America and the Caribbean, as well as the Middle East and North Africa (MENA).

> **BOX 4.1 EUROPEAN COLONISATION AND SECULAR IDEOLOGIES**
>
> Motivated by the pursuit of economic gain and the desire to spread Christian civilisation, Europe's imperial powers had spread the West's officially secular ideologies. This process continued until World War II, after which a rapid and conclusive process of decolonisation ensued. Prior to that, for a century from the mid-nineteenth to the mid-twentieth century, the vast European empires in the non-Western world – mainly run by the French and the British – had huge social, economic, political and religious impacts. Secular ideologies – such as conservatism, liberalism, communism and nationalism – found numerous new adherents around the globe. Religion, on the other hand, was typically associated with 'traditional' behaviour and resulted, according to many Western scholars and governments, in political and cultural backwardness. As Europe's erstwhile colonial possessions in the global south achieved independence, the political frameworks of new nationalist governments were typically shaped and guided by Western-derived secular political ideals. At this time, many independence movements and post-colonial nationalist governments in Asia, Africa and elsewhere in the global south found socialist and nationalist ideologies especially attractive. At the same time, the Cold War struggle raged over which Western secular ideology would prevail: liberalism/capitalism or communism. In the late 1980s, the end of the Cold War left many countries, including the erstwhile components of the Soviet empire, to look for political values and ideologies with roots in their own cultures and histories rather than those imposed from outside by Western or Eastern imperialism.

The American political scientist, Francis Fukuyama (1991), controversially proclaimed in his notable book, *The End of History and the Last Man*, that the close of the Cold War marked the world's turning away from contentious ideological competition. Fukuyama claimed that with the exception of Maoist – that is, revolutionary communist – beliefs, that at the time continued to guide the ideology of anti-state rebel groups in a few countries in the global south, including Peru and Nepal, the age of contentious politics appeared to be over; liberal democracy and capitalism had, it appeared, triumphed over radical ideologies, including communism.

Contemporaneous with what to Fukuyama appeared to be the decline and imminent demise of contentious ideological competition and conflict, various expressions of religious faith began to reassert themselves, both socially and politically, characterising a period of religious resurgence. Having been diminished in the West by the rise of secular politics and ideology and undercut globally by Western and Eastern imperialisms, many religions began to reassert themselves both publicly and politically, in effect inserting themselves into contentious political issues and seeking to influence outcomes, often via direct action, demonstrations or civil disobedience. Political and social movements in many former Western colonies, notably in Asia, Africa and the MENA region, often looked to religion to rediscover cultural identity and a political programme.

Political Islam, also referred to as Islamism, was prominent in the search for political ideologies in many Muslim-majority countries contentious. There developed a novel scholarly, policy and popular focus on the relationships between religion and contentious politics. The consequence was an expanded focus and purview – especially in terms of the depth in the scope of inquiry – to look beyond the subject of social cleavages in order to analyse the complexity and multiplicity of forms by which religion and politics interact. For example, the temporary victories of Islamist political parties, consequential to the events of the Arab Uprisings in 2011, as evidenced by the electoral successes of the Freedom and Justice Party in Egypt, Ennahda in Tunisia and the Party of Justice and Development in Morocco, collectively highlight the increased significance of the interaction of religion and politics in the MENA region, results often achieved by the use of contentious political actions, including strikes and rebellions. However, despite proclaimed adherence to the same religious faith, Islam, the rise to power of ideologically different political parties highlighted both varying religious dimensions while also underlining various ways that 'Islam' could be manifested in many ways, both politically and ideologically. This divergence served to drive the need for further research on questions of religion and ideology with regard to areas including democratisation, party platform formation, party moderation and secularisation, social constituency representation and interest articulation.

Three decades before the Arab Uprisings of the early 2010s, there was an earlier important example of the link between religion and contentious politics in another Muslim-majority country: Iran. The country's 1979 revolution provided strong evidence of how a radical religious movement using the methods of contentious politics, including direct action, demonstrations and civil disobedience, was able to overthrow a modern, secular, pro-Western regime and go on to create and consolidate in power a revolutionary religious political party, the Islamic Republic Party. Soon after, the role of the Pope and the Roman Catholic Church in supporting Solidarity in Poland during the 1980s, an organisation which used a panoply of contentious political methods to try to influence political developments in its favour, ably demonstrated the power of religion to lead a popular movement to challenge a non-democratic regime, away from authoritarianism and towards democracy.

Like the broader field of religion and politics, the study of religion and contentious politics was long circumscribed in the context of the once-dominant secularisation paradigm. For decades after World War II, modernisation and secularisation theories channelled scholarly attention away from the relationship between religion and contentious politics. Secularisation theory predicted that the importance of religion's political impact would decline as countries secularised. Contrary to secularisation theory, rather than uniformly declining in response to modernisation, there was instead a religious resurgence in many countries. Although secularisation is clearly still occurring in many, if not most, countries (Norris and Ingelhart 2004), it coexists with often widespread religious revivals (Haynes 2021). Contrary to the tenets of secularisation theory, the impact of religion on politics has not simply declined. Instead, it has changed in rather complex ways.

In the next four sections, we trace the impact of religion on four significant areas of contentious politics: democratisation and democracy, right-wing populism, culture wars and terrorism.

DEMOCRATISATION AND DEMOCRACY

Democratisation is a process of moving from an authoritarian regime to a democratically elected government. A democratic state has its governance rooted in representative institutions, with most officeholders chosen by the populace through periodic 'free and fair' local and national elections. In various ways, religion may be significant for democratisation outcomes in various ways, involving a range of possible outcomes.

The relationship between religion, democratisation and democracy centres on three issues:

- Religious traditions have core elements: some are conducive to democratisation and democracy, others less so;
- Religious traditions are typically multi-vocal: at any moment there will be powerful figures more or less receptive to and encouraging of democracy;
- Religious actors on their own rarely if ever determine democratisation outcomes.

Our starting point is to note that, around the world, religions have left their assigned place in the private sphere, becoming politically active in various ways and with assorted outcomes.

Religion's re-emergence from political marginality dates from the late 1970s. Then, as Casanova (1994: 6) notes, 'what was new and became "news" ... was the widespread and simultaneous refusal of religions to be restricted to the private sphere'.

The relationship between religion, democratisation and democracy is a crucial issue in the political life of the contemporary world. Although scholars disagree about their nature and scope, there is widespread concern in many countries regarding the role of religious actors in (1) helping underpin or support authoritarian regimes, (2) inter-communal clashes and (3) transnational extremist networks. In Europe, for example, such phenomena today represent a dual challenge: first, religious communities must effectively integrate into democratic institutions while, second, policy-makers must work out and implement new policies and forms of cooperation to cope with previously unexpected threats and issues, some of which come from religious extremist actors.

> ### BOX 4.2 POLITICS AND RELIGION IN BRAZIL
>
> Formally a secular democracy, Brazil is the largest Catholic nation not only in Latin America but in the world. The country has seen in recent years growing numbers of people converting from Catholicism to Evangelical Protestantism. These conversions provide an important example of study the interaction of religion, party politics and democracy in the Americas.
>
> In Brazil, both culture and institutions have uniquely shaped the ways in which religion involves itself in politics both historically and contemporarily. Of importance in this context are the ways that the relationship between the two main religious movements in the country, Catholicism and Evangelicalism, has affected both the evolution of politics and political party dynamics. This relationship impacts on the current institutional context and influences connections between political parties and specific religious groups, with emphasis on the role of electoral rules and Brazil's multi-party system in affecting the connection between religious groups and political parties.
>
> Modelmog and dos Santos (2019) focus on these issues in a recent paper and elaborate on the rise of what they call the 'Evangelical Caucus' in Brazil's legislature and how it affects the political process, discussing ways in which the Caucus both weakens and strengthens connections between religious groups and political parties.
>
> Modelmog and dos Santos (2019) conclude by noting that the relationship between religion and party politics has changed considerably since the return to democracy in the 1980s, during the third wave of democratisation. The 2018 election, which saw the coming to power of Jair Bolsanaro, a right-wing populist, helped to shift the relationship, with conservative Christian groups supportive of Bolsanaro's divisive political style. To understand more about the relationship between religion and politics in Brazil today, research into Brazilian party politics should include attempts to understand how 'Evangelical politicians influence party platforms, the influence of Evangelical voters and politicians (through the growing Evangelical Caucus) on majoritarian elections and coalition formation, and the ways in which the Evangelical Caucus strengthen or

> undermine party dynamics in the country' (Modelmog and dos Santos 2019: 14).

Religion can affect our world in one of two ways: by what it says and/or does. The former relates to religion's theology or doctrine. The latter refers to religion's importance as a social phenomenon and mark of identity, which can function through various modes of institutionalisation, including civil society, political society and religion-state relations. It is necessary to distinguish between religion expressed at the individual and group levels: only in the latter is it normally of importance for understanding related political outcomes.

When religion moves into the realm of politics, we are concerned with group religiosity, whose claims and pretensions are always to some degree political. That is, there is no such thing as a religion without consequences for value systems, including those affecting politics and political outcomes. Group religiosity, like politics, is a matter of collective solidarities and, frequently, of inter-group tension, competition and conflict, with a focus on either shared or disputed images of the sacred or on cultural and/or class, in short, political, issues. To complicate matters, however, such influences may well operate differently and with 'different temporalities for the same theologically defined religion in different parts of the world' (Moyser 1991: 11).

To try to bring together the relationship between religious actors, democratisation and democracy in all their varied aspects and then to try to discern significant patterns and trends is not a simple task. But, in attempting it, three points are worth emphasising. First, there is something of a distinction to be drawn between looking at the relationship in terms of the impact of religion on democratisation and democracy and vice versa. Yet, they are also interactive: one stimulates and is stimulated by the other. In other words, because we are concerned with the ways in which power is exercised in society, and the ways in which religion is involved, the relationship between religion, democratisation and democracy is both dialectical and interactive. Both causal directions need to be held in view.

Second, religions are creative and constantly changing; consequently, their relationships with democratisation and democracy can also vary over time. Finally, as political actors, religious entities can only usefully be discussed in terms of specific contexts; it is the relationship with government – whether supporting it or seeking to undermine it – which forms a common, although not the only, focal point. Yet, the model of responses, while derived from and influenced by specific aspects of particular religions, is not necessarily inherent to them. Rather this is a theoretical construct suggested by much of the literature on state-society relations, built on the understanding that religion's specific role is largely determined by a broader context.

The assumption is that there is an essential core element of religion shaping its behaviour in, for example, Christian, Islamic or Jewish societies and communities.

RIGHT-WING POPULISM

BOX 4.3 RIGHT-WING AND LEFT-WING POPULISM

Ekström, Patrona and Thornborrow (2018: 2) note that populism can be either 'left wing' or 'right wing'.[1] 'Right-wing' populism is analytically problematic. For example, many related politicians and parties, in Europe and elsewhere, prefer a social democratic-style welfare state compared to one where 'market forces' would take precedence, which is typically a 'right-wing' position. Where the designation 'right wing' comes in is that such a political approach focuses on ethnicity and religion, identifying those which the right-wing populist approves or disapproves. Often, right-wing populism, especially in Europe, is anti-Islam (Haynes 2020).

Right-wing populists may claim that there is but one 'true religion' – that is, their own and their followers' – which helps focus their political vision. Populists bring religion and culture into their arguments to encourage political changes in their favour.

Populists identify and target those they claim are 'enemies of the people', who are said to be a serious threat to fulfilment of a populist vision of a future free from culturally and religiously 'alien' influences.

Right-wing populism is a political ideology combining right-wing nationalist politics and populist rhetoric and themes. It typically comprises anti-elitist sentiments, opposition to the perceived Establishment, speaking to and for the 'common people', and a pronounced dislike of 'foreigners', which in many European countries, such as France, Hungary, Poland, the United Kingdom, as well as in the United States during the presidency of Donald Trump, are typically Muslim immigrants (Ekström, Patrona, and Thornborrow 2018; Mudde 2007; Weyland 2013).

In the West, right-wing populists typically identify their main 'enemy' as Islamist extremism, radicalism and terrorism (Haynes 2019). While Islam is vilified as a faith, Muslims generally are regarded with suspicion. Waever (2006) notes that it is fashionable to 'talk of a "clash of civilizations" between the West and Islam'. Such talk has its origins in the events of 11 September 2001 (9/11), whose outcome was a continuing concern for the West's social and political stability, leading to widespread securitisation of Islam. Waever (2006) adds that, as a result, the world may be 'standing on the brink of a long conflict, perhaps a new "cold war" that features small-scale, but spectacular violence'. Concern with escalating inter-civilisational conflict between the West and the 'Muslim world' is unquestioningly one of the key reasons for significant electoral support in many Western countries for right-wing populist nationalists. Beyond the West, for example in India and Turkey, populist nationalists have recently enjoyed electoral success (Schwörer and Romero Vidal 2020).

While right-wing populist parties are not ideologically identical, they often share significant characteristics. Right-wing populists are generally influenced by 'nationally specific factors such as political history, system and culture', and they tend to work from a similar ideological 'playbook' with the following characteristics (Greven 2016; also see DeHanas and Shterin 2018). First, their main target is an allegedly corrupt incumbent elite political class, from which the mass of the ordinary people needs defending, and for which the right-wing populist politician claims to be the saviour. Second, they claim to champion the rights and legitimacy of the Indigenous, culturally similar, 'ordinary people' against the 'immigrant-loving', self-serving business 'elites' who, they claim, want mass immigration for self-interested economic reasons: to flood the jobs market with 'foreigners' willing to work for comparatively low wages and undercut indigenous workers' salaries for bosses' profit. Huntington (2004: 268) contends that 'these transnationals have little need for national loyalty, view national boundaries as obstacles that thankfully are vanishing, and see national governments as residues from the past whose only function now is to facilitate the elite's global operations'. Third, in many European countries, including France, Germany and Italy, as well as Australia, the USA and India, right-wing populist nationalists vilify Islam as a faith and Muslims as a community. Fourth, many right-wing populists seek to invoke the alleged splendours of their purportedly superior civilisations, whether Christian (in Europe, Australia and the USA), Muslim (in Turkey) or Hindu (in India), as part of their quest for political support and votes.

Nukhet Sandal (2021) examines the rule of the ruling party, *Adalet ve Kalkınma Partisi* (Justice and Development Party, AKP) in Turkey. Sandal explains that the AKP employs religious populism in its ideological appeals, which informs the party's political strategy. She traces how the AKP, a religious populist party, has over time competed with and distinguished itself from other mainstream and conservative Turkish political actors and movements. They include the Kemalist Cumhuriyet Halk Partisi (Republican People's Party), the *Milli Gurüş* (National Outlook) movement, the *Gülen* (also known as Hizmet) movement and an 'ultranationalist' group, *Milliyetçi Hareket Partisi* (Nationalist Action Party). Each has their own interpretations of citizenship and nationalism, with Islamic populism playing a variable ideological role.

Giorgio Shani (2021) examines the relationship between rightwing populism and Hindu nationalism in India, after China, the world's most populous country. Shani focuses on the three-way relationship between Hindutva ('Hindu-ness'), religion and nationalism. Shani accounts for the development of Hindu nationalism in India as articulated by the Bharatiya Janata Party (BJP) under Prime Minister Narendra Modi. He explains that Hindu nationalism is a fusion of conservative nationalism and religion which has proved highly successful in recent years at the ballot box. The aim is a Hindu *Rashtra* or state. The idea of Hindutva is central to Hindu nationalism which considers all Indians as belonging to a Hindu civilisation based on a common pan-Indian Hindu national identity. Muslims occupy the position of a 'constitutive outside' enabling the construction of a Hindu Rashtra; they remain 'enemies' to be either excluded or assimilated to a Hindu national culture. Consequently, they remain targets of government legislation. Shani illustrates his argument by focusing on several recent important political developments in India. These include the 2019 abrogation of Article 370 which removed the special status, that is, limited autonomy, of the state of Jammu and Kashmir, the only Muslim-majority state in India; the building of a temple to the Hindu god Ram in Ayodhya, Uttar Pradesh, constructed on the site of a pre-existing mosque, and the 2019 Citizen Amendment Act, which undermined the status of some Muslims in India. Shani concludes with the claim that, under Modi, India is on the way to becoming a Hindu Rashtra, with deleterious consequences for religious minorities.

CULTURE WARS

America's political polarisation is characterised by culture wars involving the Christian Right[2] and secular conservatives, on the one hand, and religious and secular liberals, on the other. Many white Christian conservatives, both Protestant and Catholics, agreed with former president, Donald Trump, that America is a country where religion, especially Christianity, needs to be protected from secularisation. Many secular white conservatives also like what they hear when Trump proclaims he would kick start a new era of American prosperity by strictly controlling immigration and increasing availability of well-paid jobs to native Americans. Trump's neo-nationalism gave his policies focus and direction, appealing to millions of Americans, especially the 73% of the population who describe themselves as 'white'.[3] Many white Americans agree with Trump that the USA is heading in the wrong direction, both at home and internationally. Only he, they claim, can stop the rot and start a new era of American greatness (Bergmann 2020: 185–96).

In America, the longstanding consensual tradition of civil religion declined and subsequently culture wars developed. To explain what happened, we need to identify why religion retains clear political significance in the USA. Writing three decades ago, Wald (1991: 241) argued that religion is multifaceted, expressed 'through such diverse paths as the impact of sacred values on political perceptions, the growing interaction between complex religious organizations and State regulatory agencies, the role of congregational involvement in political mobilization and the functionality of Churches as a political resource for disadvantaged groups'. Wald explains that America's cultural, political and social development was greatly affected by patterns of individual and group religious commitment, which encouraged religious differentiation. This led to a growing number of extant religions in the USA, often with divisions within them. It also resulted in religious voluntarism, that is, most people believe that religious choices are not necessarily an ascriptive trait, conferred by birth. Instead, they are more a matter of choice and discretionary involvement. What is the situation today, compared to Wald's comments 30 years ago? Religious cleavages did not disappear as America modernised. Instead, they were redefined and extended to a growing number of social and political issues, expressed in the culture wars.

BOX 4.4 CIVIL RELIGION AND CULTURE WARS IN THE USA

Following World War II, America went through a long period of rising prosperity and national optimism. At this time, America was said to be characterised by 'civil religion', a consensual non-partisan allegiance to a communal religious outlook. Society was believed not to be associated with any particular political or ideological position, reflective of a shared religious and cultural tradition, which had developed over time.

The state sought to cultivate 'civil religion' as the focus of American political community. Jean-Jacques Rousseau was the first

> to use the term 'civil religion' in his *The Social Contract*, published in 1762, and subsequently Alexis de Tocqueville (1969) examined civil religion in the specific context of America. To Rousseau, civil religion was the American polity's shared religious dimension. Mainly through the work of the American sociologist, Robert Bellah, civil religion became an important concept in the modern sociology of religion. Bellah sought to define the concept as a demonstrative assertion of a shared civic faith, of great social and political significance throughout the history of post-colonial America. Bellah, in 'Civil religion in America', an influential article published in 1967, identifies civil religion as the *generalised* religion of the 'American way of life', existing with its own integrity alongside particularistic expressions of faith, including several Christian denominations and Judaism.
>
> Robbins and Anthony (1982: 10) understand civil religion as the 'complex of shared religio-political meanings that articulate a sense of common national purpose and that rationalize the needs and purposes of the broader community'. Thus, for both Bellah and Robbins and Anthony, civil religion advanced the idea that a post-colonial democratic United States was an agent of God, signifying that the American nation exhibited a collective faith serving a transcendent purpose. Political and religious spheres were constitutionally separate, and civil religion was regarded as the means to unite them, a crucial component of what it meant to be American. In recent years however, as exemplified by the divisive presidency of Donald J. Trump, the unifying concept and ideology of civil religion was superseded by the onset of America's culture wars, in which religious division played a prominent role.

Robert Bellah saw civil religion as essential to restrain the self-interested elements of American liberalism, encouraging it towards a public-spirited citizenship which enabled republican institutions to thrive. Bellah saw civil religion as a fundamental prerequisite of a stable democracy, a necessary antidote to the United States' inherently pluralistic and individualistic culture. It was the glue that held society together, the key means by which Americans arrived at common societal values in a country built, on the one hand, on ideals of mutual tolerance and unity and, on the other, on great cultural and religious diversity. Civil religion made a highly positive contribution to societal integration, exhibiting a clear ability to bind a group of diverse people, who were nevertheless united in achieving a common goal, while imparting a sacred character to citizens' civic obligations and responsibilities.

The concept of civil religion also provided a means for public manifestation of religious faith, counteracting particular religious expressions' tendency towards individuality. However, just as Bellah was proclaiming the great importance of civil religion to the integrity of the United States, the country was being torn apart by societal strife which, in hindsight, can be seen as the opening shots in today's culture wars. On the one hand, there was increasing structural differentiation of private from public sectors and, on the other, there were widening societal divisions: religious, racial, ethnic and class. Collectively, these developments undermined generalised acceptance of a shared conception of moral order. Bellah's mid-1970s book, *The Broken Covenant* (1975), argued that social changes were destroying public confidence in US intuitions, fatally weakening consensual traditions that had historically sustained faith in the republic. The societal consensus, believed central to civil religion, was effectively shattered by national reverses and scandals, including the Vietnam War and the Watergate scandal in the 1970s and early 1980s. Adding to these specific social and political travails, American unity was further undermined by polarising disputes over racial, moral and ethical issues. While the former mainly focused on the position of African-Americans and Hispanics, the latter included state prohibitions on gender- and race-based discrimination, abortion rights, increased rates of cohabitation, permissiveness towards sexual expression in art and literature, reduced sanctions against homosexuality and a Supreme Court decision proscribing school prayer.

Taken together, these developments are indicative of a decisive shift from traditional Judeo-Christian morality to a new divisiveness in the late 1960s and early 1970s, where civil religion could no longer fulfil its traditional unifying role among Americans. It led to the Moral Majority, followed by the Christian Right. As Wald (1991: 256) noted, 'if the core of the concept' of civil religion is 'the tendency to hold the nation accountable to divine standards, then the case can be made that US political culture has actually been revitalized by the rise of the "New Christian Right" (NCR)'. In 2025, rather than seeking to rebuild the consensus manifested in civil religion, the Christian Right mobilises against perceived unacceptable manifestations of liberalism, such as senior Democratic politicians, including Kamala Harris, and Black Lives Matter (BLM). Founded in 2013, BLM is a decentralised political and social movement that seeks to highlight racism, discrimination and racial inequality experienced by Black people and to promote anti-racism. For the Christian Right, BLM is a symbol of America's moral decay.

RELIGIOUS TERRORISM

Contemporary religious terrorism is relatively novel in both domestic and international politics. Yet, its impact has been significant. On the other hand, there is a previous history of terrorism and political violence of which we should be aware. Despite the contemporary importance attached to religious terrorism, it did not begin with the al Qaeda attack on the USA on 9/11. Yet, the contemporary brand of Islamist terrorism does represent something new and particularly dangerous to order and stability in international politics. We shall briefly examine the phenomenon below. Before that, we examine the historical diversity of terrorism and consider its definitional challenges in order to understand how it affects international politics.

Terminology is a significant problem when seeking to look at the issue of terrorism and political violence. Many names are attached to various political expressions and they may change over time. Notwithstanding the fact that today terrorism and political violence are closely associated with the religious extremism of al Qaeda or Daesh and, increasingly with the secular terrorism and political violence of the far right in the USA and Western Europe, terrorism as an analytical category is more complex.

What happens in the 'real world' is important for theorising about various phenomena, including terrorism and political violence. For example, Iran's Islamic revolution in 1979 led to a focus on the international effects of the country's revolution, via Iran's foreign policy. Two decades later, 9/11 renewed the West's focus — some would say obsession — with the impact of Islamic extremism and terrorism as it affected international politics, in particular stability, security and order.

Seeking to explain religious terrorism and political violence, it is useful to think beyond exclusively religious motivations for these actions and events. For Hurrell (2002: 197), it 'seems plausible that much [Muslim] resentment has to do with the far-reaching and corrosive encroachments of modernization, westernization and globalization'. Burke (2015) contends that 'if the current wave of [Islamic] militancy has its origins anywhere, it is in the religious revival across the Islamic world of the 1960s and 1970s, and the urbanisation, economic development, politics and wars that prompted it'. For both Hurrell and Burke, something in the process of 'modernisation' affects some Muslims in a certain way, encouraging them to get involved in 'Islamic terrorism'.

Key to an understanding of many 'cultural' — that is, religious and identity — factors in international relations are the activities of religious terrorists (Huntington 1996; Haynes 2019). In recent years, the most eye-catching, controversial, topical and discussed example is, as already noted, Islamic terrorism. For many observers, this was new and unexpected, in two ways. First, until quite recently, most international politics experts believed that religion could be ignored because it appeared so insignificant in the mainly secular context of world politics (Haynes 2021). Second, the end of the Cold War in the late 1980s ushered in a new era of religious involvement in international terrorism, with 9/11 a prime example. The consequence of these two developments is that today most observers of international politics would agree that it is now impossible to ignore the involvement of various 'religious actors' in many examples of contemporary terrorism.

Before proceeding, we need to engage head on with a key term: religious terrorism. We need to understand what it is and how it differs from 'non-religious' terrorism. Martin (2007: 111) explains that

> Religious terrorism is a type of political violence motivated by an absolute belief that an otherworldly power has sanctioned — and commanded — terrorist violence for the greater glory of the faith. Acts committed in the name of the faith will be forgiven by the otherworldly

power and perhaps rewarded in an afterlife. In essence, one's religious faith legitimizes violence as long as such violence is an expression of the will of one's deity.

Gregg (2014) understands religious terrorism as 'typically characterised as acts of unrestrained, irrational and indiscriminate violence, thus offering few if any policy options for counterterrorism measures'. Juergensmeyer (2017) believes, however, that

religion may not be the 'real' problem – because it does not itself *cause* the violence and terrorism associated with it. The problem, he believes, is that some may interpret their religious faith as 'allowing' them to use political violence and terrorism to achieve their god's will.

Martin and Gregg seem to agree that religious terrorism has two key dimensions. First, it may involve unconstrained political violence, and, second, it is linked to a more general rebellion against the Western liberal international order. These two characteristics highlight both the domestic and international foci of religious terrorism.

What we have discussed so far in this section should not lead us to assume *religious* terrorism is simply *Islamic* terrorism. As Haynes (2019) explains, religious terrorism is associated in recent decades with *all* the 'world faiths': Buddhism, Christianity, Hinduism, Islam and Judaism. For example, Buddhist Burmese 'ethically cleanse' Muslim Rohingyas and Buddhist Sri Lankans tortured, maimed and killed their Tamil/Hindu neighbours during the country's civil war (1983–2009). The Lord's Resistance Army in Uganda – who claimed to be Christians – spent decades energetically killing those whose views they did not like, as part of their campaign allegedly to found a political regime based on the Ten Commandments of the Bible. In India, Hindu nationalists have targeted Muslim Indians and other religious minorities in their bid to achieve a Hindu nationalist state. Finally, Jewish 'freedom fighters' in what was then Palestine bombed hotels in the 1930s and 1940s, killing in pursuit of their goal: an independent state of the Jews.

Whether religious or nonreligious, terrorism always has to do with extremist violence, or the threat of it, in pursuit of a broadly political aim. Terrorism emerged as a concept following the French Revolution of 1789, when it became a tactic of the new revolutionary state. Over time, our understanding of what terrorism is has shifted enormously, both in theory and practice. If this book had been written in the 1970s, analysis of terrorism would likely have focused on leftist rejection of Western capitalism or on separatist non-state groups in various countries, including Burma (now known as Myanmar), India or Peru. Today, however, attention has shifted to different forms of terrorism, including religious and far-right terrorism and associated political violence. In other words, what terrorism is at any one time tends to reflect what is happening in the world at any particular time. Yet, coverage is inevitably partial and our feelings about terrorism today may be less abstract than, for example, a theoretical discussion of Marxism. Many analyses of religious terrorism in the 2000s and 2010s focused on 'Islamic terrorism'. This reflected the main concern at the time in many countries' politics, as well as in relation to international politics: the religious terrorism of al Qaeda and Islamic State (sometimes known by the Arabic acronym, Daesh).[4] At the time, they were condemning vast swathes of the Middle East to instability, disorder, violence and deaths. By the mid-2020s, however, both al Qaeda and Islamic State were, if not defeated, diminished in stature, and the threat to both domestic and international order and stability appeared to have declined.

In addition to the religious terrorism of al Qaeda and Islamic State, there is today a new terrorism focus: far-right groups in the USA and Europe, who want to change the politics of their countries due to what they regard as an unacceptably high level of immigration of non-native people into their countries. While there is still much concern with Islamist terrorism and political violence, the political impact of the far right in the USA and Western Europe is significant and according to many commentators is growing. A focal point of the new concern was the mob attack on the US Capitol building on 6 January 2021, which brought the US far-right to the attention of the world's media and analysts.

Twenty years earlier, the al Qaeda attacks on the World Trade Centre and the Pentagon on 11 September 2001 (9/11) propelled religious terrorism to international attention (see 'The 9/11 Commission Report' (http://govinfo.library.unt.edu/911/report/911Report_Exec.htm). Over the next two decades, wars, bombs, attacks, civilian deaths, downed airliners, as well as numerous deaths of American, British, Afghan, Iraqi, Syrian soldiers and civilians, were graphic evidence of the challenges posed by religious terrorism. After 9/11, many in the West saw themselves at war – for example, the then US President, George W. Bush, proclaimed that America was leading a 'Global War on Terror' – fighting against Islamist extremism and terrorism, notably Al-Qaeda and Islamic State/Daesh (Haynes, 2019).

A consequence of 9/11 and its aftermath – especially, the US-led 'war on terror' and increasing securitisation of Islam (Haynes, 2019) – was an increased focus on religious *ideas*, especially Islamist extremism and terrorism. It also led to a renewed focus on Samuel Huntington's (1996) 'clash of civilisations paradigm, which focused on 'The West' and 'Islam' as radically different concepts, informed by dissimilar ideas and values. Each was constituted in relation to state power and mobilised for the purpose of sustaining system-transforming political projects. This was done either by Western liberal democracies, whose aim was to redefine sovereignty and global governance norms, and by religious terrorist organisations seeking to do the same but with different aims.

CONCLUSION

This chapter has explained that in today's world relationships between religion and politics sometimes may move beyond the realm of everyday political discourse to include what are known as 'contentious politics'.

After defining and explaining what are the key issues involved in contentious politics, the chapter examines the issue of religion in relation to contentious politics, describing how it may be linked to areas of significant political and social contestation. We looked at four issues in some detail in the chapter for two reasons, first, religious involvement is pronounced, and, second, religions have been used in various ways to try to get the outcomes that activists wish to see. The focused upon areas were democratisation and democracy, right-wing populism, culture wars and religious terrorism.

QUESTIONS

1. What are contentious politics and how is religion involved in them?
2. Why is religious involvement in democratisation and democracy a contentious issue?
3. How are right-wing religious populism and religion linked?
4. What is the role of religion in America's culture wars?
5. Why is Islam commonly associated with religious terrorism?

NOTES

1 Several populist parties in Europe, such as Syriza in Greece and Podemos in Spain, as well as the self-proclaimed 'socialist' Bernie Sanders Senator in the USA, fall into the category of 'left-wing' populism.
2 The Christian Right, sometimes referred to as the Religious Right, is a collection of Christian political factions characterised by their strong support of socially conservative and traditionalist policies. Christian conservatives in the USA seek to influence politics and public policy with their interpretation of the teachings of Christianity.
3 'White people constitute the majority of the U.S. population, with a total of about 234,370,202 or 73% of the population as of 2017' (https://en.wikipedia.org/wiki/Demographics_of_the_United_States).
4 Daesh is an acronym for *al-Dawla al-Islamiya fi al-Iraq wa al-Sham*: D *dawlat* = state in English, A or I = Iraq, e = and SH = *al-Sham*, a term for a region encompassing Syria and Lebanon.

RECOMMENDED READINGS

Adib Abdulmajid, *Sectarian Roots of Jihad: Religious Conflicts in the Middle East*, New York: Lexington Books, 2014. Abdulmajid examines the sectarian dimension of *jihad* and delves into the under-researched sectarian-inspired discursive employment of the notion by radical Islamist groups.

Tobias Cremer, *The Godless Crusade: Religion, Populism and Right-Wing Identity Politics in the West*, Cambridge: Cambridge University Press, paperback edition, 2023. Cremer explores how right-wing populists use religion as a cultural identity marker against minorities, while remaining distanced from Christian values, beliefs and institutions

Daniel Nilsson DeHanas, and Marat Shterin (eds.), *Religion and the Rise of Populism*, London: Routledge, 2020. After 2016, following the US presidential election and the Brexit debate in the United Kingdom, populism took centre stage in global discussions on democracy. This book aims to correct the oversight that, while religion plays a key role in populism in many countries, it is often overlooked in academic debates.

Jeffrey Haynes, *Trump and the Politics of Neo-Nationalism: The Christian Right and Secular Nationalism in America*, London: Routledge, 2021. The author explains the links between Trump and the Christian Right which was an important factor in the outcome of the 2016 presidential election in the USA.

ONLINE RESOURCES

Democracy Network. https://democracynetwork.org.uk/resources/

Digital Culture Wars. www.eurozine.com/digital-culture-wars-far-right-powerbase/

European Centre for Populism Studies. www.populismstudies.org/Vocabulary/digital-populism/

University Module Series. Introduction To International Terrorism. www.unodc.org/documents/e4j/18-04932_CT_Mod_01_ebook_FINALpdf.pdf

REFERENCES

Bergmann, Eirikur. 2020. *Neo-Nationalism. The Rise of Nativist Populism*. London: Palgrave Macmillan.

Burke, Jason. 2015. 'There is no silver bullet': ISIS, Al Qaida and the myths of terrorism', *The Guardian*, 20 August. www.theguardian.com/world/2015/aug/19/isis-al-qaida-myths-terrorism-war-mistakes-9-11

Casanova, José. 1994. *Public Religions in the Modern World*. Chicago and London: University of Chicago Press.

DeHanas, Daniel Nilsson, and Marat Shterin. 2018. 'Religion and the rise of populism', *Religion, State and Society*, 46, 3: 177–85.

Dos Santos, Pedro, and Linsey Modelmog. 2019. *Religion and Political Parties in Brazil*. College of Saint Benedict and Saint John's University, Political Science Faculty Publications. https://digitalcommons.csbsju.edu/cgi/viewcontent.cgi?article=1071&context=polsci_pubs

Ekström, Mats, Marianna Patrona, and Joanna Thornborrow. 2018. 'Right-wing populism and the dynamics of style: A discourse-analytic perspective on mediated political performances', *Palgrave Communications*, 4, 83: 1–11.

Fukuyama, Francis. 1991. *The End of History and the Last Man*. New York: The Free Press.

Gregg, Heather S. 2014. 'Defining and distinguishing secular and religious terrorism', *Perspectives on Terrorism*, 8, 2: 36–51.

Greven, Thomas. 2016. *The Rise of Right-Wing Populism in Europe and the United States. A Comparative Perspective*. Washington, DC: Friedrich Ebert Foundation.

Haynes, Jeffrey. 2019. *From Huntington to Trump: Thirty Years of the Clash of Civilizations*. New York: Lexington Books.

Haynes, Jeffrey. 2020. 'Right-wing populism and religion in Europe and the USA', special issue, 'Religion, nationalism and populism across the north/south divide religion', guest edited by Jocelyne Cesari, *Religions*, 2020. www.mdpi.com/2077-1444/11/10/490

Haynes, Jeffrey (ed.). 2021. *Handbook on Religion and International Relations*. London: Edward Elgar.

Huntington, Samuel. 1996. *The Clash of Civilizations*. New York: Simon and Schuster.

Huntington, Samuel. 2004. *Who Are We? The Challenges to America's National Identity*. New York: Simon & Schuster.

Hurrell, Andrew. 2002. '"There are no rules" (George W. Bush): International order after September 11', *International Relations*, 16, 2: 185–204.

Juergensmeyer, Mark. 2017. *Terror in the Mind of God. The Global Rise of Religious Violence*. Berkeley, CA: University of California Press.

Martin, Gus. 2007. *Understanding Terrorism: Challenges, Perspectives and Issues*. New York: Sage.

Moyser, George (ed.). 1991. *Religion and Politics in the Modern World*. London: Routledge.

Mudde, Cas. 2007. *Populist Radical Right Parties in Europe*. Cambridge: Cambridge University Press.

Norris, Pippa, and Ronald Inglehart. 2004. *Sacred and Secular. Religion and Politics Worldwide*. Cambridge: Cambridge University Press.

Robbins, T., and D. Anthony (eds.). 1982. *In God We Trust New Patterns of Religious Pluralism in America*. New Brunswick: Transaction.

Sandal, Nukhet. 2021. 'Religious populist parties, nationalisms, and strategies of competition: The case of the AK Party in Turkey', *Religion, State & Society*, 49, 3: 248–63.

Schwörer, J., and X. Romero-Vidal. 2020. 'Radical right populism and religion: Mapping parties' religious communication in Western Europe', *Religion, State & Society*, 48, 1: 4–21.

Scott, James. C. 1985. *Weapons of the Weak. Everyday Forms of Peasant Resistance*. New Haven, CT: Yale University Press.

Shani, Giorgio. 2021. 'Towards a Hindu *Rashtra*: *Hindutva*, religion, and nationalism in India', *Religion, State & Society*, 49, 3: 264–80.

Tilly, Charles. 2015. *Contentious Politics*. New York: Oxford University Press

Tocqueville, Alexis de. 1969. *Democracy in America*. Garden City, NY: Doubleday.

Wald, Kenneth. 1991. 'Social change and political response the silent religious cleavage in North America', in George Moyser (ed.), *Religion and Politics in the Modern World*. London: Routledge, 239–84.

Waever, O. 2006. 'Fear and faith: Religion as an international security issue', Lecture at the Mershon Center, Ohio State University. https://kb.osu.edu/bitstream/handle/1811/30197/Ole%20W%c3%a6ver%205-17-06.pdf?sequence=4

Weyland, Kurt. 2013. 'Latin America's authoritarian drift: The threat from the populist left', *Journal of Democracy*, 24, 3: 18–32.

GENDER AND FEMINISM

> **INTRODUCTORY BOX : QUESTIONS ABOUT FEMINISM AND RELIGION**
> - How and why did feminist thought – in its various forms – come to inform analyses of religion and politics?
> - How did the liberal feminist agenda of sexual equality advance in analyses of religion and politics, while still having some way to go to achieve this ambition?
> - How has the social construction of gender and patriarchy informed analyses of religion and politics and how has feminist thinking sought to redress this?

GENDER AND POLITICS

Around the world, females' social and political position is typically subservient to that of males. This is because societal structures and processes typically reflect a common, near-universal, position: females are widely regarded – especially by men – as 'second class' citizens, with less power and authority. The issue of females' power and authority in relation to men is now widely debated (although rarely, it appears, resolved). Today, gender equality issues are an important aspect of politics, raised at all levels of political thinking, both within countries and internationally. Seeking to explain strengths and weaknesses in relation to the position of females in countries around the world, this chapter examines religious and cultural norms in relation to gender differences, political socialisation and adult gender roles.

For many years, both political science and international politics were frequently taught and theorised as if females were invisible. The implication is that there were no important women in domestic or international politics, both of which were regarded as the domain of males. It also implied that both females and males were active in and affected by politics in the same ways. As a result, there would be no need to 'gender' analysis. Things are however changing, consequent to the development of a well-established area of feminist scholarship in both political science and international politics (see, for example, True and Mintrom 2001). The result is that we now have abundant 'feminist understandings', while 'women's organizing provide us with perspectives that contribute a more inclusive view of' females' roles in relation both to politics and religion (Pettman 2001: 582).

Feminist agendas typically focus upon the general, lesser political and societal position of women compared to men. Much feminist research focuses on how women can operationalise their self-determination in relation to political, economic and social roles. A growing number of political theorists explicitly consider the issue of gender equality when comparatively assessing the nature of individual political systems and international politics. It is now common for contemporary theories of politics to relate explicitly to gender issues. However, feminist scholars still critique the mainstream majority of both comparative politics and international politics analysis for their high degree of 'gender-blindness' (Dahan-Kalev 2003). Gender-blindness relates to the fact that even today some political theories have little or nothing to say about the participation of females in politics, including transitions to and consolidation of democracy and, more generally, the still-gendered nature – of political structures and processes.

Away from the analytical mainstream, assessments of women's involvement in political processes – including democratic transitions – are now both extensive and varied, having increased significantly in recent decades (Rai 2005). Many authors of gendered analyses see their work as lying directly within the discipline of politics and the sub-discipline of comparative politics.

GENDER, POWER AND IDEOLOGY

Females face two key problems when seeking to improve their political position. The first is the difficulty of securing an enhanced public role, especially in conservative societies characterised by religious cultures which traditionally consign females exclusively to the domestic sphere as home-makers and child-rearers. The second is the importance, more generally, for women to adopt activist roles in civil society, including in religious organisations, to help achieve feminist goals (Rai 2005).

We begin this section with a brief discussion of the interconnections of religion and gender in relation to power and ideology. These issues are central to religious perceptions of the gendered position of females.

Gender-based prejudice is prevalent throughout much of the world, despite legal and other measures to overcome inequalities. More than two decades ago, the World Bank (2001: 117) stated that to improve matters, 'extra efforts' must be made 'to raise awareness about culturally based attitudes ... towards women'. This is because 'values, norms and social institutions' that traditionally privilege men can also serve to reinforce persistent inequalities between males and females that in turn can become the basis of severe deprivation and conflict'. Relevant cultural attitudes in this context include those linked to religion.

It is not clear the extent to which things have improved since the World Bank commented on the issue a quarter of a century ago. Part of the reason is that fundamental reforms are often very slow to develop and frequently depend to a significant extent on the views of those in power moving towards a more gendered focus. In addition, while scholars engaging in the academic study of religion now pay increasing attention to gender dimensions, not all aspects are yet well understood or sufficiently linked (Aune and Nyhagen 2016).

To contextualise the discussion, we need first to ascertain the role that religion plays in many women's lives. Second, we look at the issue of religious women's female agency, including female activism in religious ideological movements. Third, we assess the role of religion and gender ideologies in recent and current examples of right-wing populism in Europe and elsewhere as well as in the recent rise of authoritarianism more generally. We follow this with a brief focus on what is known as the 'anti-gender ideology' movement, a movement strongly related to both conservative political and religious figures. Finally, we note the current use of gender-equality rhetoric in mobilisations against the 'religious other', that is, Muslim migrants and minorities, in many Western countries.

POWER

Linda Woodhead (2012), a British sociologist of religion, argues that a useful starting point for any scholarly discussion about issues of gender and religion is to note that both are inherently about embodying, distributing and representing power. This is because power is fundamental to how society is structured.

Woodhead (2012) also points out that religious ideologies, practices and institutions are a constitutive part of gender orders. This is because they play a key role in ordering gender relations. For example, religion can both confirm and provide grounds of legitimation for an existing societal gender order. Or, it can challenge this order and seek proactively to institute meaningful changes, including reversal of embedded gender orders. The implication is that is the existence of normatively progressive religious movements and ideologies is helpful in advancing gender equality.

The Australian sociologists, Raewyn Connell and Rebecca Pearse (2015), argue that gender orders are intricate, socially and historically constructed systems of power relations. They are legitimised in various ways, including by institutions, structures and everyday actions. As a result, relations between women and men are ordered, reordered and made concrete in society.

Reza Aslan (2017), an Iranian-American scholar of sociology, argues that all three monotheistic religions – Christianity, Islam and

Judaism – tend to try to humanise the divine. This is despite the emphasis in Islam that the divine has no image, substance or form. Nevertheless, the Islamic idea is typically that God is a male figure, a supposition that underlines the centrality of gender orders in religious ideologies and their link to secular sources of gendered power.

IDEOLOGY

Religions are sometimes referred to as comprehensive or 'thick' ideologies. A thick ideology is one that 'offers a comprehensive program of political change' and has 'staying power' (Schroeder 2020). Elements of feminism, which collectively advance the idea of human equality independent of gender, and nativism, that is, the belief that nation-states should be exclusively filled by natives and that non-natives threaten the nation, are said to be 'thin', that is, less comprehensive, ideologies.

'Thick' ideologies have the following characteristics:

- significant internal integration
- a comprehensive core linked to a substantial range of political concepts
- ability to express a large range of concepts and political positions
- comprehensive answers to sociopolitical questions
- far-reaching objectives and scope
- a sufficiently cohesive and intricate 'ideological product'
- relative unity among actors cohering around the 'thick' ideology (Freeden 1996, cit. after Aslanidis 2016: 64)

'Thin' ideologies offer a less comprehensive set of answers to sociopolitical questions. As the Greek political scientist, Paris Aslanidis (2016) argues, the frequent ambiguity of the definition of ideology in the social sciences, including in political science and international politics, can make a hard-and-fast distinction between thick and thin ideologies rather difficult to determine. On the other hand, despite shortcomings, these concepts are still helpful in distinguishing between full-fledged – that is, 'thick' – ideologies and more fragmented or less comprehensive sets of political thought, that is, 'thin' ideologies.

Both ideology and power are in mind in relation to the controversial issue of females' sexual and reproductive health rights (SRHR), a topic which takes the attention of many religious, as well as secular, authorities. The issue became of international significance following a series of high-profile, United Nations (UN)-sponsored, international conferences between 1992 and 2000. The UN conferences focused on the following topics, which collectively drew attention to the lack of power of females, especially in relation to gendered human rights (Vienna, 1992), the natural environment (Rio, 1992), population (Cairo, 1994), human development (Copenhagen, 1995), women and gender (Beijing, 1995) and social development (Geneva, 2000). The cumulative effect was to shift both domestic and international agendas from the relatively uncontroversial area of 'women's issues', a 'thin' ideological issue, to a 'thicker', more comprehensive set of gendered concerns, collectively involving cultural, political, economic, social, environmental and military issues.

Each of the UN conferences had a focus on human rights and social justice and collectively they were significant for a concern with how to improve the social and developmental position of females, especially in the global south. However, despite the intention of bringing in a new world order, the conferences were chiefly notable for a fundamental lack of international agreement on what steps to take – and what resources to devote – to resolve pressing human rights and social justice problems. Overall, persuasive evidence emerged not of a wide-ranging consensus for improvement but instead its opposite: often intense disagreement, with views dividing along ideological lines, pitting conservatives against liberals, bringing together secular and faith-based entities and state and non-state actors.

BOX 5.1 WOMEN'S SEXUAL AND REPRODUCTIVE HEALTH RIGHTS AT THE UNITED NATIONS

Sexual and reproductive health rights (SRHR) are a controversial issue at the United Nations (UN). The SRHR controversy at the UN is emblematic of divisions between normatively conservative and liberal views on human rights and social justice, disputes that

> are played out but seemingly never resolved, which involve both religious and secular power holders. On the one hand, there is the 'unborn's right to exist', while on the other hand, there is a woman's right to do with her body as she sees fit.
>
> It is impossible definitively to claim ethically that one view is 'right' or 'wrong'. How we see the SRHR issue is linked explicitly to our normative understanding of what is right and wrong. In recent decades, the issue – that is, women's human rights versus those of the unborn child – has become a major international controversy, and while not all scholars would agree that the issue is of central to understanding international politics, related activism is now an important component of transnational relations involving religion. The 1994 UN Cairo Conference was pivotal in this development. The Cairo conference was organised to discuss, on the one hand, the best and most appropriate methods of birth control – in the context of a swiftly growing global population putting an intense and growing strain on environmental resources – and, on the other, the issue of how to arrive at more 'female-friendly' definitions of human rights in a global context where females' rights in many countries are marginalised or ignored (Haynes 2014).

Controversy attaching to these issues was highlighted by the decision of the Holy See, using its status as permanent observer at the UN, to 'delay the discussion of reproductive "rights" of women and to mobilize sympathetic states (including Saudi Arabia and Sudan) against voluntary choice in family planning' (Sandal 2012: 72). The Holy See, also referred to as the See of Rome, Petrine See or Apostolic See, is the central governing body of the Catholic Church and the Vatican City State.

Neither Saudi Arabia or Sudan has significant Catholic populations – Saudi Arabia's Christian population is officially zero while that of Sudan is around 5%, with most of the remainder being Sunni Muslims. It is evident that the campaign led by the Holy See was not faith-based. Rather, it emphasised a shared conservative worldview in relation to women's human rights, involving both the leader of the Roman Catholic Church and Saudi Arabia, a Muslim-majority theocracy. At Cairo, the position of the Holy See led Egypt's then population minister, Maher Mahran, to state in exasperation: 'We respect the Vatican. We respect the Pope. But if they are not going to negotiate, why did they come?' (Mahran quoted in Sandal 2012: 72). Both Egypt and Saudi Arabia are majority Sunni Muslim countries and their division on this issue illustrates that their shared faith did not mean that both countries' governments – neither of which at the time were democratically elected – regard women's SRHR in the same way. In sum, the 'unholy' alliance of the Holy See, Saudi Arabia and Sudan on this issue illustrates that something other than a shared faith view facilitated their cooperation. It was a common, normatively conservative perception, which transcended faith, that the human rights of women do not extend to control over their own bodies when it comes to reproductive health and reproductive rights.

BOX 5.2 EXCLUSION OF (THE STUDY OF) RELIGION IN LATIN AMERICAN GENDER STUDIES

According to Vuola (2015), contemporary scholarship on women and gender in Latin America is often guided by a twofold relationship to religion. First, religion is not seen or, even less, analysed as a factor in women's lives. Vuola (2015) calls this 'feminist blindness to the importance of religion, especially in its aspects that women might experience as positive and life-sustaining'.

Second, when feminist scholars of Latin America do take religion into account, typically they do so through what Vuola (2015) identifies as a religious paradigm or 'religion-as-a-lens type of theorizing. Here, religion is seen as the main explanatory factor of women's lives in a given culture, regarded as uniformly negative, misogynist, and as an unchallengeable force. Yet, such a depiction does not necessarily take women's own interpretations into account, nor does it interpret "religion" as lived religion, shaped by people, but rather as an institution'.

Moreover, there is a strong tendency in feminist Latin American studies to see all established religion, including popular Catholicism, as harmful and alienating for women. The main woman in the eyes of the Catholic Church, the Virgin Mary, is widely seen as a role model for females. When women love Mary, feminist scholars see their devotion as the worst sort of alienation. This is known as the *marianismo* thesis. In addition, little differentiation is

> made between institutional, official religion, on the one hand, and lived religious practices, on the other.
>
> In Latin American studies, exclusion of religion and related studies (such as anthropology, religious studies and theology) is especially emphasised in gender studies. This is problematic, not least because issues related to gender, women, family and sexual ethics are central to religion's interaction with the secular world, not only in Latin America but also more generally.
>
> Why do some social scientists not take religion seriously in gender studies? Partly, it is due to a paucity of knowledge of research done in fields such as religious studies and theology. Partly, it is because of understanding religion rather narrowly. In the specific case of Latin America, there is a specific institutional academic situation whereby religion is studied either in seminaries, institutions and universities of different churches, or as a theme among others in fields such as anthropology, history and political science. Consequently, the academic field of the study of religion in Latin America differs from that of the United States or Western Europe, where the study of religion, including theology, is part of secular universities' curricula. This exclusion of religion – understood critically, broadly and from the perspective of various disciplines – is partly a result of the relative lack of scientific study of religion in Latin America and helps to explain the lack of social scientific concern with the relationship between religion and gender in the region.

ISLAMIC FEMINISM

During the 1990s, women's empowerment, not only in relation to SRHR but also more generally, became an important global topic. Like elsewhere, this was also the position in the Muslim world. At this time, 'Islamic feminism' emerged as a focal point to assess the societal position of females in Muslim countries.

Islamic feminism is both discourse and practice, articulated in what is referred to as an 'Islamic paradigm'. In the Islamic paradigm, Islamic feminism derives its understanding and mandate not from secular Western theories but from the Muslim holy book, the *Qur'an*, which offers comprehensive guidance on rights and justice for both women and men.

Islamic feminism is firmly embraced by some, mainly female, Muslims and highly contested by others because of its controversial objective: equality for females in Muslim-majority societies. Islamic feminism starts from the understanding that only rarely do women hold public positions of authority in most Muslim-majority societies. According to Reveyrand-Coulon (1993: 97), this indicates that Muslim women typically constitute a 'subordinated group'. In many Muslim-majority societies, many men expect women to remain at home to run domestic affairs and rear children, and not seek a more prominent role in society and politics. Both cultural and social factors inhibit women in many Muslim-majority countries from organising meaningfully in pursuit of collective self-interest. Such factors help to explain especially egregious examples of the subordination of Muslim females in several countries, including Afghanistan, Iran, Iraq, Jordan and Saudi Arabia.

Several egregious examples of what Reveyrand-Coulon (1993) refers to female subjugation can be briefly noted. First, in Muslim-majority Iraq in 1990, a proclamation was issued by the then-ruling Revolutionary Command Council, announcing that 'any Iraqi (male) who kills *even with pre-meditation* his own mother, daughter, sister, niece, or cousin for adultery will not be brought to justice' (emphasis added; Ekins 1992: 76). A second example is from Jordan, a Muslim-majority kingdom torn between strict religious and ethnic traditions and swift modernisation. In Jordan, at least a quarter of all premeditated murders are so-called honour killings: male relatives murder female members of their family for so-called immoral behaviour, such as 'flirting' and losing virginity before marriage (Sabbagh 1994). Third, in March 2002 in Mecca, Saudi Arabia, 50 schoolgirls were burned to death and dozens more injured in a fire at their school. Religious police are said to have 'prevented the girls from leaving the building because they were not wearing headscarves, and had no male relatives to receive them. They also reportedly prevented rescuers who were men from entering the premises' (Amnesty International 2004: 1).

In these examples from Iraq, Jordan and Saudi Arabia, Islam is a common factor which helps to explain cultural attitudes towards females, including a generally lowly position for females in many Muslim countries. The American scholar, Jane Parpart (1988: 209), claims that the influence of Islam, especially 'through purdah or ritual seclusion', serves to constrain 'female economic and political activities'. On the other hand, it should be noted that because interpretations of Islam differ from country to country, then links between the status of females and the faith are necessarily both complex and varied. The American scholar, David Held (1993: 23), explains that, in addition, various factors, including 'regime ideology, power relations within the family, low literacy rates and employment opportunities … play a determining role'.

BOX 5.3 SIGNIFICANT CHALLENGES FACING ARAB/MUSLIM WOMEN

According to the Secretary General of Religions for Peace, Azza Karam, women in Arab countries,[1] most of whom are Muslim, face five significant challenges when trying to improve their political, economic and social position:

1. *Economic position*: Many Arab women are both poor and illiterate. These factors comprise major hurdles in Arab women's attempts both to spread awareness and to access necessary opportunities for social and political development.
2. *Culture*: Cultural factors are important, especially the idea that an Arab woman's place is in the home. In addition, most existing political institutions suggest the existence of a male-dominated and male-oriented culture.
3. *Freedom of association*: Many Arab women face problems linked to freedom of association. This can seriously affect ability to organise, especially in the NGO sector, reducing the ability for Arab women to 'network' both within their own countries and internationally.
4. *Political parties*: Men dominate most political parties, and their interests and concerns reflect this fact.
5. *The media*: The role the media plays in Arab countries in promoting the interests of women and of female politicians is problematic (Karam 1998: 3).

Arab/Muslim females do not necessarily accept conditions of subservience passively. Over time, Islamic feminism has gained increased visibility. From the 1990s, Islamic feminists sought to increase awareness of Muslim women's typically lowly societal and political status position and seek ways to improve them. Afsaneh Najmabadi (2005) and Ziba Mir-Hosseini (2019) note an increase in the use of the term Islamic feminism in a theocracy, Iran, including articles and op-eds by women published in a Tehran-based feminist journal, *Zanan*, which commenced publication in 1992. In addition, a Saudi Arabian scholar, Mai Yamani (1996), also uses the term in her book, *Feminism and Islam*. Finally, three Turkish scholars, Yesim Arat (2000), Nayereh Tohidi (2007) and Nilufer Gole (1997), use the term Islamic feminism in their writings to describe a new feminist paradigm they detect in Turkey. In sum, from the mid-1990s, there is increasing use of the term 'Islamic feminism' in several Muslim countries.

The term Islamic feminism has two meanings. On the one hand, it is an analytical term, while on the other it is a term of identity. Some Muslim women regard Islamic feminism as a project of articulation and advocacy of the practice of gender equality and social justice as mandated by the *Qur'an*. Others do not call this Islamic feminism *per se* but describe it as an Islamic project of rereading the *Qur'an*, women-centred readings of religious texts, or what Webb (1999) calls 'scholarship-activism'.

BOX 5.4 ISLAMIC FEMINIST DISCOURSE

How is Islamic feminist discourse organised? Islamic feminist discourse includes what some Muslims refer to as 'Islamic feminist theology' ('Islamic feminism means justice to women' 2004). The basic argument of Islamic feminism is that the *Qur'an* affirms the principle of equality of all human beings but that the practice of equality of women and men (and other categories of people) has been impeded or subverted by patriarchal ideas and practices. Islamic jurisprudence, *fiqh*, was consolidated in its classical form over a thousand years ago, in the ninth century. Reflecting the concerns of the time, it was heavily informed with patriarchal thinking and behaviours. This patriarchally dominated jurisprudence in turn informed various formulations of the *Shari'a* (Islamic law).

Apart from the Muslim holy book, the *Qur'an*, there is a second authoritative source in Islam: the *hadith*, which comprises the reported sayings and deeds of the chief prophet of Islam, the Prophet Mohammed. Like *fiqh*, *hadiths* have often been used to shore up patriarchal ideas and practices. Some are of questionable provenance or reliability, and sometimes they are used out of context. For Islamic feminists, as a result, it is necessary to go directly to Islam's fundamental and central holy text, the *Qur'an*, in an effort to find its egalitarian message, not necessarily to rely upon *fiqh* or *hadiths*.

To examine the impact of Islamic feminism further, we look at the positions of females in Muslim-majority Turkey and Christian-majority France.

TURKEY AND ISLAMIC FEMINISM

In July 2006, Turkey's religious authorities declared that they would remove the following statements, and more like them, from the *hadiths*:

- 'Women are imperfect in intellect and religion'
- 'The best of women are those who are like sheep'
- 'If a woman doesn't satisfy her husband's desires, she should choose herself a place in hell'
- 'If a husband's body is covered with pus and his wife licks it clean, she still wouldn't have paid her dues'
- 'Your prayer will be invalid if a donkey, black dog or a woman passes in front of you'

Over 90% of the *Shari'a* is based on *hadiths* rather than the *Qur'an* itself. Indeed, many of its most controversial strictures — including, killing of apostates, seclusion of women, ban on fine arts and stoning of adulterers — emanate from the *hadiths* and subsequent commentaries — all of which were written by male religious authorities. To remove such statements from the *hadiths* is a direct challenge to some of the most controversial aspects of Islamic tradition (Akyol 2016).

Turkey's highest Islamic authority, the Diyanet, proposed the revisions. The Diyanet controls over 75,000 mosques, both in Turkey and among Turkish communities in various European countries, such as Germany, which has a large Turkish population. The Diyanet's president, Ali Bardakcioglu, is a liberal theologian who was appointed in 2003 by the ruling Justice and Development Party. Bardakcioglu (2004) not only declared that a new collection of *hadiths* would be prepared by 2008 but also announced that less tradition-focused imams would be sent to the rural, conservative regions of South East Turkey to preach against practices, such as honour killings, that explicitly target women.

Hidayet Tuksal, a doctor in Islamic theology and the author of a critical study of the gender bias in *hadith* (Tuksal 2001), has expressed unease about inconsistencies and narrow-minded assertions contained in the *hadiths*. However, the issue is complicated. Other *hadiths* explain Mohammed's great respect for his wives, for example, and insist on the rights of women. Tuksal notes that this contradiction needs to be resolved, stating that 'I can't imagine a prophet who bullies women …. The hadiths that portray him so should be abandoned' (Tuksal quoted in Akyol 2016).

Tuksal has written a history of the Islamist women's movement in Turkey, which includes an account of the dual struggle of Turkish women for their rights as both committed Muslims and as women. In an effort to develop an Islamic discourse that is liberating, Tuksal (2001) argues that Islamic feminists have been up against the state as well as Muslim men, both secular conservative and Islamist. In Turkey, Tuksal (2001) reports, there is no convergence, as there is in Iran, between secular and Islamic feminism. In Turkey, secular feminists are rarely interested in their Islamist sisters' struggles for rights, and when they do support a case it is usually presented as proving the essentially oppressive nature of Islam.

Tuksal describes herself as a 'religious feminist'. Born in 1963, and holder of a PhD in Islamic theology from Ankara University, Tuksal is a leading figure in a new generation of Islamic feminists advocating gender equality. She was one of the founders of the Capital Women's Platform (*Baskent Kadin Platform*) in 1994 in

Ankara. The platform sought to draw attention to injustices and discrimination that religious women suffer in secular circles. It also challenged the religious basis of traditions that discriminate against women. As Tuksal (2001) notes: 'Religion has been interpreted differently by different people throughout history, leading to male-dominated interpretations'. She argues that progress will come as a result of collaboration among different women's groups:

> Many women opposing the headscarf are academics who come from university women's research departments. But even they reached the point saying 'Come and let us talk about the headscarf in a closed meeting.' They never said that before. Socialist feminists and women with headscarves sit next to each other.
>
> (European Stability Initiative 2007)

Overall, the reform process in Turkey highlights one of the basic methodologies of Islamic feminism: classic Islamic methodologies of *ijtihad* (independent investigation of religious sources), and *tafsir* (interpretation of the *Qur'an*). Used along with these methodologies are various methods and tools, including those of linguistics, history, literary criticism, sociology and anthropology. In approaching the *Qur'an*, Islamic feminists in Turkey women bring to their readings their own experiences and questions as females. The conclusion is that in both classical and most postclassical interpretations of Islam, commentaries and judgements are based on men's experiences, seek to deal with male-centred questions and are strongly informed by the patriarchal societies which produced them.

FRANCE AND ISLAMIC FEMINISM

France is home to more than 5 million Muslim inhabitants, nearly a tenth of the population. It is thought that about 50% have French citizenship – although precise figures are unavailable. This is because the French state is officially secular and officials do not ask French people questions about their religion or lack of it. Many observers would agree, however, that while still preponderantly Catholic, France now has more Muslims than Jews or Protestants, historically the country's most significant religious minorities.

Islam may be the country's second religion in terms of the numbers of followers.

Growth in the numbers of Muslims in France came initially by immigration. Many came from France's former North African colonies, including Algeria and Morocco. Although a presence from around the time of World War I, Muslims arrived in significant numbers in France from the 1960s. At this time, the government granted asylum to hundreds of thousands of Algerians who had fought on the French side in Algeria's 1954–62 war of independence. During the same decade, France also invited immigrant manpower – including Muslims – to meet the needs of a then-booming economy. The economic boom fizzled out in the 1970s, but by then there were Muslims in most of France's population centres.

France has had a policy of 'zero immigration' since the 1970s. However, France's Muslim population still increases because of relatively high birth rates, an unknown number of illegal entrants, from sub-Saharan Africa and elsewhere, and a legal exception that allows the reunion of immigrant families. The purpose of the exception makes clear French policy in regard to its Muslims: to legitimise them by integrating them into French society.

Successive French governments have sought to integrate Muslims into the existing society. This has implied reducing overt signs of 'Muslim-ness', especially particularistic forms of dress, such as the hijab ('Islamic veil'). The so-called headscarves of Creil affair erupted in late 1989 and focused on the desire of several young Muslim women to wear Islamic headscarves at school in the seaside town of Creil. The affair was portrayed in the French media as an attempt to introduce 'communalism' into schools, a traditionally neutral sphere. To explain the passion that this issue has raised we need to be aware that France is the country where the Enlightenment began, a development characterised by a strong conviction that the common ground for the French is 'rationality'. This implies that religion takes a secondary position. Many French people are highly secular and perceive visible signs of religious identity – such as the hijab – as highly disturbing because they believe it undermines basic French values.

Around this time in France, Islamic networks were growing, made up primarily of students and other young people, often from the Maghreb. Some wanted to stage a trial of strength by confronting the French state on the sensitive ground of laïcité (i.e. 'secularism'). The issue seemed to strike a chord with many French Muslims who, it appeared, also wanted 'positive discrimination' in favour of Muslim girls in French state schools. The student militants appointed themselves as the spokespeople of 'Islam' and sought to negotiate 'positive discrimination' for practising Muslims that would allow them to withdraw, in some areas, from the laws of the Republic and instead obey *sharia* law. The Islamic militants found powerful allies, including the hierarchy of the Roman Catholic Church and some Jewish rabbis. Such religious figures supported them because they too were determined to seek a renewal of their faiths in the face of laïcité. Eventually, after a long campaign, the French national assembly voted overwhelmingly in February 2004 in favour of a ban on Islamic veils in state schools, despite new warnings from religious leaders that the law would persecute Muslims and encourage fundamentalism. MPs voted 494–36 in favour of banning 'conspicuous' religious symbols in schools. The law, ratified by the Senate in March, came into effect in September 2004.

The European Network against Racism (ENAR) reports that Muslim females in France are discriminated against in various ways. The ENAR recommends the following to reduce or remove discrimination against Muslim females in France, including in relation to employment opportunities:

- Include a gender focus in the French national action plan against racism in order to better address the multiple discrimination affecting women from ethnic and religious minorities and recognise Islamophobia as a specific form of racism.
- Establish a qualitative and quantitative balanced assessment of the 2010 legislation prohibiting the concealment of the face in public spaces, including an assessment of its abusive use against Muslim women.
- Stop any attempts to extend religious neutrality to the public space or any private spaces such as companies.

- Take concrete measures to ease the collection and monitoring of equality data (disaggregated by gender) based on perceptions and self-perceptions of the interviewees.
- Identify common concepts to encourage convergence between feminist and anti-racist organisations against common discrimination and violence.
- Initiate training sessions on anti-discrimination legislation for employers and trade unions.
- Boost the Diversity Label to sustain involvement of companies and institutions in the programme and include public authorities in this process (www.enar-eu.org/wp-content/uploads/factsheet_france_-_en.pdf).

CONCLUSION

The chapter began by asserting that, nearly everywhere, females' social and political position is subservient to that of males. We saw that this is commonly but due to widespread societal structures and processes which reinforce a common, near-universal, position: females are widely regarded – especially by men – as 'second class' citizens – indicating both a lack of power and authority. We also saw that today the issue of females' power and authority in relation to men is now widely debated (although rarely, it appears, resolved), focused in various understandings of religious feminism. Over time, gender equality issues have become an important aspect of politics, raised at all levels of political thinking, both within countries and internationally, including at the world's leading international organisation, the UN. Seeking to explain strengths and weaknesses in relation to the position of females in countries around the world, the chapter examined religious and cultural norms in relation to gender differences, political socialisation and adult gender roles.

Illustrating the concerns of the chapter, we included brief case studies of women's SRHR at the UN, Islamic feminism, the exclusion of (the study of) religion in Latin American gender studies, and the religious and social position of females in a Muslim-majority country, Turkey, and a Christian-majority country, France. Overall, the chapter demonstrated that the relationship between religion and gender in many parts of the world is both a controversial topic and one that women are trying their best in many ways to improve.

QUESTIONS

1. What is Islamic feminism?
2. Why does Latin America have a lack of focus on the role of women in politics?
3. Why are sexual and reproductive health rights a controversial issue at the United Nations?
4. How does the societal position of Muslim women in Turkey and France differ?
5. What do females need to do to improve their societal and political position, including in relation to men's religious domination?

NOTE

1 Arab countries have their own international organisation, the League of Arab States. The League of Arab States was founded in Cairo, Egypt, on 22 March 1945, following adoption of the Alexandria Protocol the previous year. The League's current headquarters are in Cairo, Egypt, and its membership includes 22 Arab states. All are Muslim-majority countries located in the Middle East and North Africa. Member states are Algeria, Bahrain, Comoros, Djibouti, Egypt, Iraq, Jordan, Kuwait, Lebanon, Libya, Mauritania, Morocco, Oman, Palestine, Qatar, Saudi Arabia, Somalia, Sudan, Syria, Tunisia, the United Arab Emirates and Yemen.

RECOMMENDED READINGS

Arash Azizi, *What Iranians Want: Women, Life, Freedom*, London: Bloomsbury, 2025. Azizi guides us through recent events in Iran. From an International Women's Day celebrated inside Iran's most notorious prison to mass strikes in Kurdistan, ordinary Iranians are taking risks to fight for a better future. Azizi explains that a different Iran is within sight.

V. G. Julie Rajan, *Women, Violence, and the Islamic State: Resurrecting the Caliphate through Femicide*, London: Routledge, 2025. This book explores the self-proclaimed Islamic State's (IS) perspectives on and violence against women.

Meredith Whitnah, *Faith and the Fragility of Justice: Responses to Gender-Based Violence in South Africa*, New Brunswick: Rutgers University Press, 2025. South Africa often makes news headlines because of its high rates of gender-based violence. In the midst of a wide range of responses to the problem, an important voice has been largely absent. The book explains why religious groups, which had famously protested the racial violence of apartheid, faltering in their response to gendered violence in the country.

ONLINE RESOURCES

Feminism and Religion (FER) Online School. 'The approach is primarily intended for those who look to academically question their beliefs, attitudes, knowledge and practices about human rights and freedoms and who want to research how gender stereotypes shape the lives of women and men in the family and society.' https://eiz.hr/en/training/feminism-and-religion-fer-online-school/

Feminist Studies in Religion. 'Feminist Studies in Religion, Inc. (FSR, Inc.) is a 501(c)(3) nonprofit educational organization whose goal is to foster feminist studies in religion in all of its variety and diversity. We understand "feminist studies in religion" to encompass global critical feminist work in religious studies, theology, and spirituality both inside and outside the academy and at the grassroots level. We seek to generate new feminist scholarship in religion that is intersectional and committed to social justice, and to create spaces for such scholarship to emerge. Founded in 1983, FSR, Inc. pioneered the development of feminist studies in religion as a field through its establishment and sponsorship of the *Journal of Feminist Studies in Religion*.' www.fsrinc.org/about-fsr/

Religion and Gender: Religion and Women. 'Religions really don't seem to do very well when it comes to women and equality. Equality is usually understood to mean both equality of value and equality of opportunity. So we say that a human boy is of the same value as a human girl. Gender does not make one greater or lesser. In modern thinking, the belief that we all share an equal human value should lead to everyone having the same opportunities, especially when it comes to questions of power and authority.' www.reonline.org.uk/knowledge/16-ethics/religion-and-gender-religion-and-women/

REFERENCES

Akyol, Mustafa. 2016. 'Why is Turkey reviving an Ottoman sultan?', *Al-Monitor*, September 29. Accessed 3 January 2017. www.al-monitor.com/pulse/originals/2016/09/turkey-reviving-sultan-abdulhamid-ii.html

Amnesty International. 2004. 'It's in our hands. Stop violence against women'. www.amnesty.ie/wp-content/uploads/2016/05/Its-in-our-Hands.pdf

Arat, Yesim. 2000. 'Gender and citizenship in Turkey', in S. Joseph (ed.), *Gender and Citizenship in the Middle East*, Syracuse: Syracuse University Press, 275–86.

Aslan, Reza. 2017. *God. A Human History*. New York: Random House.

Aslanidis, Paris. 2016. 'Is populism an ideology? A refutation and a new perspective', *Political Studies*, 64, 1: 88–104.

Aune, Kristin, and Line Nyhagen. 2016. 'Religion, politics and gender', in Jeffrey Haynes (ed.), *Handbook of Religion and Politics*, 2nd ed. London: Routledge, 335–51.

Bardakcioglu, A. 2004. 'The Republic of Turkey Presidency of Religious Affairs Press and Human Relations Office Press Release, March 8, World Women's Day'. www.diyanet.gov.tr/en-us

Connell, Raewyn, and Rebecca Pearse. 2015. *Gender: In World Perspective*. Cambridge: Polity.

Dahan-Kalev, D. 2003. 'The gender blindness of good theorists: An Israeli case study', *Journal of International Women's Studies*, 4, 3: 126–47.

Ekins, Paul. 1992. *A New World Order. Grassroots Movements for Global Change*. London: Routledge.

European Stability Initiative, PICTURE STORY. A century of feminism in Turkey. June 2007. www.esiweb.org/pdf/esi_picture_story_-_a_century_of_feminism_in_turkey_-_june_2007.pdf. Accessed 4 April 2025.

Gole, Nilufer. 1997. *The Forbidden Modern: Civilization and Veiling*. Ann Arbor: University of Michigan Press.

Haynes, Jeffrey. 2014. *Faith-Based Organizations at the United Nations*. New York: Palgrave Macmillan.

Held, David. 1993. 'Democracy from city-states to a cosmopolitan order?', in David Held (ed.), *Prospects for Democracy*. Cambridge: Polity, 13–52.

'Islamic feminism means justice to women'. 2004. Published in the 16–31 January 2004 print edition of *The Milli Gazette* ('Indian Muslims' leading English newspaper'). Available at www.milligazette.com/Archives/2004/16-31Jan04-Print-Edition/1631200425.htm

Karam, Azza. 1998. *Women, Islamisms and the State: Contemporary Feminisms in Egypt*. Basingstoke: Palgrave Macmillan.

Mir-Hosseini, Ziba. 2019. 'The challenges of Islamic feminism', *Gender a výzkum/Gender and Research*, 20, 2: 108–22.

Najmabadi, Afsaneh. 2005. *Women with Mustaches and Men without Beards*. Gender and Sexual Anxieties of Iranian Modernity. Berkeley: University of California Press.

Parpart, Jane. 1988. 'Women and the state in Africa', in Donald Rothchild and Naomi Chazan (eds.), *The Precarious Balance. State and Society in Africa*. Boulder: Westview, 208–30.

Pettman, Jan Jindy. 2001. 'Gender issues', in John Baylis and Steve Smith (eds.), *The Globalization of World Politics. An Introduction to International Relations*, Oxford: Oxford University Press, 582–98.

Rai, Shirin. 2005. 'Gender and development', in Jeffrey Haynes (ed.), *Palgrave Advances in Development Studies*, Basingstoke: Palgrave Macmillan, 226–46.

Reveyrand-Coulon, Odie. 1993. 'Les enoncés féminins de l'islam', in Jean-Francois Bayart (ed.), *Religion and Modernité. Politique en Afrique Noire*. Paris: Karthala, 63–100.

Sabbagh, Rana. 1994. 'Jordanian women pay the violent price of traditional male "honour"', *The Guardian*, 28 December.

Sandal, Nukhet. 2012. 'The clash of public theologies?: Rethinking the concept of religion in global politics', *Alternatives*, 37, 1: 66–83.

Schroeder, Ralph. 2020. 'The dangerous myth of populism as a thin ideology', *Populism*, 3, 1: 13–28.

The World Bank. 2001. *World Development Report 2000/2001*. New York: Oxford University Press.

Tohidi, Nayareh. 2007. 'Muslim feminism and Islamic reformation', in R. Radford (ed.), *Feminist Theologies: Legacy and Prospect*, Minneapolis: Fortress Press, 93–116.

True, Jacqui, and Michael Mintrom. 2001. 'Transnational networks and policy diffusion: The case of gender mainstreaming', *International Studies Quarterly*, 45, 1: 27–57.

Tuksal, Hidayet Şefkatli. 2001. *Kadn Karst Soylemin Islan Gelenegindeki Izdusumleri*. Ankara: Kitabiyat.

Vuola, Elina. 2015. 'The exclusion of (the study of) religion in Latin American gender studies', *LASA Forum*, 46, 1: 17–19.

Webb, G. (ed.). 1999. *Windows of Faith: Muslim Women's Scholar Activists in North America*. Syracuse: Syracuse University Press.

Woodhead, Linda. 2012. *Religion and Change in Modern Britain*. London: Routledge.

Yamani, Mai. 1996. *Feminism and Islam. Legal and literary perspectives*. Reading, UK: Ithaca Press.

FREEDOM AND DISCRIMINATION

STATE POLICIES WITH RESPECT TO FREEDOM OF RELIGION OR BELIEF

Human rights are a key concern of the United Nations (UN) organisation. After World War II ended in 1945, human rights were seen as pivotal in international attempts to build international mechanisms of cooperation. The UN has maintained an interest in human rights and today the range of human rights with which the international organisation is concerned has grown to include the rights of the religious in an increasingly secular world. The issue of international religious freedom is today of major importance, a topic given focus following its inclusion from the 1990s as a major and consistent aspect of United States foreign policy. Originally expressed in the American Constitution of 1788, religious freedom has long been a foundational component of America's culture and values, and this concern now includes the USA's international politics.

> ### INTRODUCTORY BOX : ELEANOR ROOSEVELT AND HUMAN RIGHTS
>
> Eleanor Roosevelt served as First Lady of the United States from 4 March 1933 to 12 April 1945, during her husband President Franklin D. Roosevelt's unprecedented four terms in office. Roosevelt was a

> lifelong Protestant Christian, a member of the Episcopalian church and regularly attended church services (Glendon 2010). Eleanor Roosevelt was not only the longest-serving First Lady of the United States but was also chair of the United Nations Human Rights Commission, instrumental in the creation of the UDHR.
>
> During World War II, the US government portrayed the 'Christian' West's fight against fascism/Nazism as an international struggle between 'good' and 'evil'. In 1948, leading American Christians, notably the then-first lady, Eleanor Roosevelt, were instrumental in crafting the Universal Declaration of Human Rights, a fundamental document of the United Nations.

Initial UN concerns with human rights were expressed in a major international agreement: the 1948 Universal Declaration of Human Rights (UDHR). The human right to freedom of religion or belief (FoRB) was first articulated in the preamble to the UDHR, which declares the 'advent of a world in which human beings shall enjoy freedom of speech and belief and freedom from fear and want [...] as the highest aspiration of the common people' (www.un.org/en/about-us/universal-declaration-of-human-rights).

'Freedom of religion or belief' establishes 'the right of every individual to have, adopt, or change a religion or belief; to manifest and practice this religion or belief; to be free from coercion and discrimination on the grounds of this religion or belief; and to ensure the religious and moral education of their children'. The right to FoRB was set out in Article 18 of the UDHR, which focused on freedom of thought, conscience and religion. In addition, the right to non-discrimination on the grounds of religion or belief was covered in Articles 2 and 7 of the UDHR (Petersen 2021).

A subsequent international agreement, the International Covenant on Civil and Political Rights (ICCPR) was signed in 1966, becoming operational a decade later in 1976. The ICCPR not only underlines the importance of freedom of 'thought, conscience and religion' but also reaffirms rights originally articulated in the UDHR. In addition, the International Covenant adds a further right: persons belonging to religious minorities must be allowed to profess and practice their own religion freely.

Despite lengthy international efforts to draft a legally binding convention on religious discrimination, parallel to the work of the International Convention on Elimination of All Forms of Racial Discrimination (effective from 1969, which commits UN members to the elimination of racial discrimination and the promotion of understanding among all races), a similar convention on religious discrimination has not yet appeared. The best we currently have is a non-binding declaration from 1981, the Declaration on the Elimination of All Forms of Intolerance and Discrimination Based on Religion or Belief. This led in 1986 to the creation of a UN Special Rapporteur to oversee governments' voluntary implementation of the 1981 Declaration. UN Special Rapporteurs are independent experts who are responsible for monitoring specific human rights under the aegis of the UN.

The right freely to adopt, change, practice and be educated in a religion or belief assumes particular importance in the context of religious minorities striving to assert their individuality in contexts where there is a situation where a government seeks to deny or limit their rights. While there is – at least formally – considerable international consensus around the need to fight religiously related discrimination and violations of FoRB in relation to religious minorities, significant uncertainties exist as to what exactly the right to FoRB entails (Fox 2020).

Away from the UN, the issue of religious freedom has a long history in international politics. It was an important aspect of the extreme ideological discord between the USA and the Soviet Union during the Cold War, that is, from the late 1940s to the late 1980s. During this time, America's ideological battle with the Soviet Union pitched the USA's Christian culture against the USSR's 'God-less' one. After the Cold War, US foreign policy prioritised human rights, including religious freedom, democracy, and anti-slavery and human trafficking (Haynes, Hough and Pilbeam 2023).

Following the end of the Cold War in the late 1980s, the issue of international religious freedom became a key concern for both religious and secular human rights advocacy groups in the USA (Haynes 2008). Initially, the Bill Clinton administration seemed indifferent to the issue of international religious freedom (Bettiza 2019). To seek to change its position, an alliance of human rights advocacy groups successfully lobbied Congress and other arms of government. Consequently, President Clinton signed into law the International Religious Freedom Act (IRFA) in 1998.[1] The aim of IRFA is to 'condemn violations of religious freedom, and to promote, and to assist other governments in the promotion of, the fundamental right to freedom of religion.' IRFA identifies international religious freedom a core aim of America's foreign policy.

Following the Clinton presidency, subsequent presidents, George W. Bush and Barack Obama, pursued IRF policies with 'an implicit Christian soft spot', that is, allegedly favouring Christianity over other religions. During the recent presidency of Donald Trump (2017–21), 'attention to Christian concerns and communities [became] even more overt and explicit' (Bettiza 2019: 223).

The Trump administration's policy on IRF was characterised both by its enthusiasm and by a distinctive ideological position. An ideological focus was especially notable from April 2018, when Mike Pompeo was appointed as Secretary of State. Pompeo, an evangelical Christian, applied a Judeo-Christian division perspective to America's IRF policy, which emphasised Pompeo's personal view that religious freedom is first among human rights (Casey 2017, 2020; Stewart 2020). Pompeo's approach was viewed with alarm by mainstream human rights advocacy groups, both religious and secular. While they did not disagree on the desirability of international religious freedom, they questioned Pompeo's Judeo-Christian approach (Verma 2020).

BOX 6.1 THE UNITED STATES COMMISSION ON INTERNATIONAL RELIGIOUS FREEDOM

The United States Commission on International Religious Freedom (USCIRF) was established by America's International Religious Freedom Act of 1998. USCIRF publishes an authoritative annual report on international religious freedom. The purpose of USCIRF is to advance international freedom of religion or belief in line with the Universal Declaration of Human Rights. USCIRF's annual report

> highlights two categories of countries of concern: 'Countries of Particular Concern' and those on a 'Special Watch List'. The 2022 USCIRF report identified 15 in the former category and 12 in the latter.
>
> The US president appoints USCIRF Commissioners, following consultation with the leaderships of both main political parties, Democrats and Republicans, in the Senate and the House of Representatives. USCIRF produces annual reports highlighting particularly egregious examples of repression of religious minorities' rights in countries around the world. The USCIRF reports are the closest thing the international community has to an authoritative overview of religious minorities' rights around the world. The issue is of consistent concern in relation to some countries, where the freedoms of some religious minorities are consistently threatened by their governments (Haynes 2020).

INTERNATIONAL RELIGIOUS FREEDOM AFTER WORLD WAR II

Beyond the USA, the issues of religious freedom and discrimination against religious minorities are topics of great international concern. There are two main aspects of the issue of international religious freedom and equality: legal and normative aspects. The existential situation of religious minorities varies greatly from country to country and from culture to culture, and there is an array of legal and normative relationships regarding religious minorities in states' domestic policies (Fox 2020).

Religious freedom is problematic for many religious minorities in countries around the world. Religious minorities seek to preserve or enhance their religious, cultural and/or ethnic characteristics and have done so since the global spread of nation-states from the eighteenth century. The increase in the number of nation-states following the Peace of Westphalia in 1648, from a small handful to around 200 today, gradually consolidated the dominance of secular over religious power holders, while also downgrading the public significance of many religious entities, which formerly had had a central position. Subsequently, European imperialism and colonialism disseminated Western-style, secular governments throughout much of the global south.

After World War I, there was increased international recognition and attempts to protect minorities' rights under international law. This was especially in relation to minority peoples' attempts to create their own nation-states in opposition to colonial administrations. The forerunner to the UN, the League of Nations, established in 1919, adopted various 'minority treaties', including in relation to religious minorities. Following the defeats of both Germany and the Turkish Ottoman Empire in World War I, both lost their colonial territories in the Middle East, Africa and the Pacific. Under the League of Nations' 'mandates', the former colonies of Germany and the Ottoman Empire were administered by a number of countries, including the United Kingdom and France (Cesari 2021).

Replacing the League of Nations in 1945, the UN established several norms, procedures and mechanisms seeking to protect the rights of minorities, including religious minorities. In addition to the previously mentioned 1966 International Covenant on Civil and Political Rights, further UN measures included the 1992 Declaration on the Rights of Persons Belonging to National or Ethnic, Religious and Linguistic Minorities (hereafter: 'UN Minorities Declaration'). The UN Minorities Declaration recognises and seeks to protect the rights of people belonging to religious and ethnic minorities. In practice, however, these rights are far from being recognised uniformly in countries around the world.

The UN recognises the frequently dire position of refugees and other internally displaced persons, who are often victims of conflicts within many countries. Such people are often from religious minorities who find themselves persecuted because of their faith. As a result, they may lack access to, among other things, adequate housing, land and property, or even a nationality (Minority Rights 2010).

Despite rising international concern about the plight of religious minorities in many countries around the world, there is no international consensus on how to define *religious minority*. This lack of agreement is reflected in the fact that none of the major international organisations, such as the UN, or important regional entities, such as the European Union, incorporate a definition of religious minority in their constitutions or formative arrangements. Yet, while the issue is contested, both historical and contemporary usage by various international actors, including governments, diplomats, policy makers, scholars and human rights activists, indicates that in the international legal context, the concept of *religious minority* is generally restricted to persons and/or groups characterised by a particular set of perceived characteristics, including religious difference, which frequently overlaps with both ethnic and cultural differences (Hannum 2018).

Effectively to promote and protect the rights of minority peoples, including religious minorities, requires attention to various issues. These include recognition of minorities' existence and guaranteeing their rights to non-discrimination and equality; local and national promotion of multicultural and intercultural education; promotion of minorities' participation in all aspects of public, including political, life; addressing minorities' concerns in relation to, including poverty-reduction measures; seeking to deal with egregious disparities in important social indicators, such as employment, health and housing and, finally, the position of women and children belonging to minorities. This is of course quite a lengthy, albeit necessary, 'list' of demands and the record of international protection of religious and ethnic minorities is both patchy and varied. In some countries, minorities are persecuted by the state, often governed by those predominantly from a majority or dominant religion. In addition, minorities are prone to be victims of armed conflicts and internal strife, including civil wars, in countries around the world, notably in the global south (Minority Rights 2010).

STATE DISCRIMINATION AGAINST RELIGIOUS MINORITIES IN THE MIDDLE EAST AND NORTH AFRICA

The recent political rise of right-wing populism in many European countries, which we looked at in a previous chapter, has brought increasing attention to religious minorities, especially Muslims, people who are frequently targets of right-wing populist discrimination. This is now a regional trend in much of Europe, which seriously threatens equality of treatment of religious minorities, notably Muslim communities. In many European countries, right-wing populists claim that Muslims are not desirable citizens because of their different faith and culture (Haynes 2019).

Europe is not, however, alone in discriminating against religious minorities. A neighbouring region, the Middle East and North Africa (MENA), provides further examples of states which consistently discriminate against some religious minorities. The United States Commission on International Religious Freedom's 2024 report identifies several MENA countries, including Algeria, Egypt, Iran, Iraq, Syria, Turkey and Saudi Arabia, which USCIRF accuses of having policies of state discrimination against Christian minorities. For example, the government of Saudi Arabia not only enforces strict limitations on all forms of expression of Christianity, including public acts of worship, but also seeks to prevent private Christian services held in individual Christians' homes (www.uscirf.gov/countries/2024-recommendations).

At the same time, several MENA states have impressive records of religious diversity, that is, environments where Muslims, Christians, Jews and others have long lived together in relative harmony, often exhibiting a significant degree of religious tolerance. Today, however, there is growing international concern, noted in the annual USCIRF reports, regarding the contemporary position of some religious minorities, notably Christians, in many MENA countries. The human rights of religious minorities in the MENA have often been considered through the lens of FoRB. However, as Ghanea (2008), notes, relevant though this analytical framework is, 'promoting the rights of the Middle East's religious minorities through the framework of minority rights may provide a more promising avenue for their protection'. Even though minority rights provisions apply to members of minorities alongside all other human rights – among them FoRB – the two lenses of minority rights and FoRB highlight somewhat different provisions and protections. The two are certainly not mutually exclusive or in contradiction with one another, but a state that prioritises one set of legal and policy options over the other will arrive in different places.

> ### BOX 6.2 JACOB MUNDY AND TRANSFORMATIVE MINORITY POLITICS IN THE MENA
>
> An American political scientist, Jacob Mundy (2010), examines in his book 'transformative minority politics' in relation to Algeria and more generally the MENA region. For Mundy, transformative minority politics is the key to strengthen democratic reforms in the countries of the MENA region, including a deepening and embedding of a culture of human rights and democratic citizenship which extends to religious minorities. Mundy identifies several religious minorities who do not currently enjoy full democratic or human rights. Among them are a North African minority, the Amazigh, also referred to as 'Berbers' and 'Imazighen'. The Amazigh live in the Maghreb region of North Africa, specifically in Morocco, Algeria, Tunisia and Libya, and to a lesser extent Mauritania, northern Mali and northern Niger. Smaller Amazigh communities are also found in Burkina Faso and Egypt's Siwa Oasis. The Amazigh's traditional religion is dominated by solar and lunar deities, which are very similar to those worshipped by the Egyptians in pre-Islamic times. In a region where Islam is the majority religion, the Amazigh are persecuted because they follow a different, pre-Islam, religion.
>
> In addition to the Amazigh, other religious and ethnic groups in the MENA also face discrimination. They include Christian Copts in Egypt, Kurds in Iraq and other MENA countries, Palestinians in Israel, Shia minorities in Syria and Bahrain, and various ethnic and religious minorities in Iran, including Ahwazi Arabs, Azeris, Bahá'is, Baluchis, Christians and Kurds.

Discrimination against religious minorities in the MENA region reflects the impact not only of current state polices but also of historical and international issues. Together, they affect the likelihood of developing a new era of transformative minority politics in the MENA, while emphasising societally and politically powerful elements that may constrain its development. The

'Arab Uprisings' of the early 2010s raised expectations that the MENA region would imminently undergo a democratic revolution, in which the rights of religious minorities would be consistently respected. This was seen as especially important in the regional rise in sectarianism which not only threatens human rights of religious minorities, but also causes serious economic problems, while leading to foreign policy meddling by various regional powers, notably Saudi Arabia and Iran.

Despite the coming together of people from all faiths in protests that led to the (temporary) demise of authoritarian governments in Egypt and Tunisia governments in the 2010s, both countries subsequently have seen increased sectarian tensions and conflict. For example, Egypt experienced attacks against Christian Coptic churches, as well clashes between Copts and Muslims, during which several people were killed. Tunisia saw the murder of a Polish-born Catholic priest, Father Marek Rybinski, killed on the premises of an inter-denominational school in Tunis, while Islamist protesters gathered outside the Great Synagogue of Tunis and a chapel was burned near the city of Gabes. In Bahrain, political violence pitted Shias against Sunnis. In Syria the Assad-led Alawite minority government blatantly exploited the country's latent sectarian divisions, trying to stabilise its hold on power, and the result is the country's still unresolved civil war. Overall, state persecution of religious minorities in several countries of the MENA reflects wider societal and political upheavals which first openly appeared in the Arab Spring events of the early 2010s, and which over time have developed in some countries into systematic human rights denials of some religious minorities (Haynes 2013).

The position of Jews in the MENA region is a long-standing controversy, which is sometimes expressed through the lens of anti-semitism. Anti-semitism, defined as hostility to, prejudice towards, or discrimination against Jews, has long been a deeply entrenched issue in the MENA. Following the 7 October 2023 attack by Hamas against Israel, there was a high degree of anti-semitic rhetoric, including on various social media platforms. Many anti-Jewish slurs came from people in the MENA. Why was this the case? Can anti-semitism in the Middle East be successfully addressed in order to lessen it? ('Antisemitism in the Middle East: Unpacking the Root Causes and Implications for Regional Stability' 2023).

A recent book, *Why Do People Discriminate against Jews*, co-authored by the Israeli political scientist, Jonathan Fox, and the interdisciplinary researcher, Lev Torpor (2021), provides a data-rich analysis of the causes of anti-semitism not only in the MENA but also more widely. Using the tools of comparative political science, Fox and Torpor examine data from 76 countries around the globe to identify causes of both state-based and societal anti-Jewish discrimination. They indicate that while anti-semitism is an attitude, discrimination against Jews involves concrete actions. Explaining the causes of discrimination, Fox and Torpor employ both ideas and theories from classic studies of anti-semitism with more recent social scientific theories. They explain that, on the one hand, conspiracy theories, a major topic in the anti-semitism literature, are relatively unexplored in the social science literature as a potential instigator of discrimination. In addition, they identify how social scientific theories, developed to explain how some governments justify discrimination against Muslims in Europe and elsewhere, are not regularly applied to similar processes leading to anti-semitism and anti-Jewish discrimination. Overall, Fox and Torpor (2021) identify three potential causes of anti-Jewish discrimination in the MENA and more widely (1) religious causes, (2) anti-Zionism, that is, against the belief that Jews should have their own state and (3) belief in conspiracy theories regarding Jewish power and attempts at 'world domination'.

INTERNATIONAL DISCRIMINATION AGAINST WOMEN AND SEXUAL MINORITIES

FoRB emerged as a key concern of the international community in the 1990s, a time when religious freedom was under attack in many countries (Fox 2020). At around the same time, the issue of equal rights for lesbian, gay, bisexual, transgender and queer (LGBTQ) people became internationally contentious, including in the United States, where it became enmeshed in the wider issue of human rights and religious freedom.

BOX 6.3 DONALD TRUMP AND CHRISTIAN CONSERVATIVE GROUPS AT THE UNITED NATIONS

One of the early acts of the 2017–21 Donald Trump administration in the USA was to reinstate what was known as the 'Mexico City policy', also referred to as the 'global gag rule'. This prevented US government support for international family planning programmes that 'perform, promote or offer information about abortion'. In addition, the Trump administration worked industriously at the UN to remove all references to 'sexual and reproductive health', the term preferred by mainstream human rights activists (Bob 2019).

Trump administration appointees worked internationally to insert anti-LGBTQ views into US foreign policy. For example, at the 2019 Commission on the Status of Women (CSW) at the UN, the US delegation attempted to remove 'gender-responsive' language from CSW exit documents. The then-US Ambassador at the UN, Cherith Norman Chalet, stated in a speech at the event that 'we are not about gender jargon ... we are about women and girls'. Some saw this as an effort to weaken the rights of non-binary individuals, in line with the Trump administration's broader attacks on the LGBTQ community, which were strongly supported by the Christian Right (Ford 2019, Verma 2020).

The then US Secretary of State, Mike Pompeo, stated his opposition to same-sex marriage in July 2018 during his confirmation hearing before the Senate Foreign Relations Committee. Sarah Kate Ellis, president and chief executive officer of the LGBTQ rights group, Gay & Lesbian Alliance Against Defamation, stated that 'Mike Pompeo's reaffirmed opposition to marriage equality and LGBTQ rights further proves that he is dangerously wrong to serve as our nation's chief diplomat .... His personal ties to anti-LGBTQ hate groups and clear refusal to support the hard-fought equal rights of the LGBTQ community make him wholly unqualified to promote human rights abroad' (Brammer 2018).

Gevisser (2020) remarks that 'during his presidency, Donald Trump has rolled back transgender rights as part of his efforts to consolidate his conservative Evangelical base, for whom "gender ideology" has become the new evil; the latest bulwark against assaults on "the family" now that same-sex marriage was legal and supported by a majority of Americans' (Gevisser quoted in Tóibín 2020).

> These examples make it clear that the Trump presidency encouraged Christian conservative groups in the USA to extend their focus internationally in pursuit of what some regarded as anti-woman and anti-sexual minority policies. The policy came to an end following the presidential inauguration of Joe Biden in January 2021.

Like the USA, Poland has religion-linked concerns about the rights of women and the country's LGBTQ community. Poland is a strongly Roman Catholic country. About 90% of Poles are Catholic, and a considerable number are practising Catholics. During the Trump presidency in the USA, the government of Poland, strongly expressing adhesion to 'traditional' – that is, highly conservative – Catholic values, supported a Christian conservative approach to women's and LGBTQ rights.

Poland held a presidential election in early July 2020. The winner was Andrzej Duda, first elected as president in 2015. Duda is a friend and ally of President Trump, and a practising Roman Catholic, who often takes part in Catholic religious ceremonies including Midnight Mass, the blessing of food on Holy Saturday and the Corpus Christi procession in the Polish city of Kraków. Still president in 2025, Duda remains a vociferous critic of LGBTQ rights, pledging to 'defend children from LGBTQ ideology' (FP Editors 2019).

Religious and secular human rights advocacy groups raise concerns about minorities, both domestically and at international fora, including the UN (Haynes 2008).

Internationally, a prominent US-based Christian conservative group, Focus on the Family, lobbies against the rights of LGBTQ people at the UN. Focus on the Family highlights the importance of what it calls 'family values', claiming that LGBTQ people undermine societal adhesion to traditional marriage, involving one man and one woman, who marry, it is claimed, primarily to have children. In general, Christian conservatives ally with their Islamic counterparts at the UN, claiming that there is a sustained, international 'liberal' attack on traditional 'family values' and attacking LGBTQ people in this context.

Attacks on LGBTQ rights at the UN from religious conservatives came to a head in 2003 when a Brazil-sponsored UN resolution presented to a UN Human Rights Commission meeting in Geneva the proposition that homosexuals should have equal rights with heterosexuals. The Brazilian government's aim was to develop the notion of human rights as a universal right for all people, regardless of sexual orientation. Brazil's resolution expressed 'deep concern' at violations based on sexual orientation and declared that 'enjoyment' of human rights should not be 'hindered in any way' by a person's sexual orientation. Brazil's move prompted the conservative coalition into swift action, and the proposition was not accepted (Haynes 2014).

DISCRIMINATION AGAINST THE NON-RELIGIOUS IN SUB-SAHARAN AFRICA

An eminent Kenyan-born Christian philosopher and writer, John Mbiti (1975) stated that 'Africans are notoriously religious'. Unlike many countries in Western Europe, there is no sign that Africa is secularising. Most Africans are followers of either Christianity or Islam.

BOX 6.4 RELIGION AND POLITICS IN GHANA

Religion is a very prominent feature of public life in the West African country of Ghana, a country with a population of more than 30 million people. Christianity, the majority religion followed by around 70% of Ghanaians, seeps into every aspect of life, including political decision-making. The country's 1992 'secular' constitution accords religion a prominent public role in the life of the country. In the context of the 1992 constitution, 'secular' means that no religion is favoured over others; it does not mean that society is atheistic or without religion.

The first line of the preamble to Ghana's 1992 constitution states that the constitution is made in the name of 'Almighty God' (https://judicial.gov.gh/index.php/preamble). The constitution states that religious liberty is guaranteed: 'All citizens are free to believe and manifest any religious faith' or none. Finally,

> the constitution 'prohibits the elevation of any religious organization into a State religion (see article 56 of the 1992 Constitution)' (Quashigah 2010: 331–2).
>
> Representatives of the country's major religious traditions, notably Christianity and to an extent Islam, followed by around 20% of Ghanaians, are included in national decision-making. This is manifested via religious figures' membership of national bodies, including state commissions, committees and national boards, such as the National Peace Council and the National Media Commission. Religion more generally plays a significant role in Ghana's public sphere, featuring prominently in state functions and in parliament where proceedings begin and end with Christian prayers. In sum, Ghana is a constitutionally secular state where religion is publicly prominent (Quashigah 2010: 331–2).

Some African governments discriminate against religious non-believers, and in some countries, they are persecuted. Both state and non-state agents are responsible for stigmatisation of and discrimination against religious non-believers in sub-Saharan Africa. While, stigmatisation, defined as the action of describing or regarding someone or something as worthy of disgrace or great disapproval, has long characterised the approach of many sub-Saharan African governments to religious non-believers, the situation has recently got worse in some regional countries. There seems not to be one particular cause of increased stigmatisation, although it seems likely that a widespread African concern is that the West is believed to be forcing culturally inappropriate views on African countries, seen as a general trigger for increased stigmatisation of religious non-believers.

The means and venues used to perpetuate stigmatisation of religious non-believers and increase their human insecurity, include discursive frames, use of traditional and social media employing disinformation campaigns, legal-political narratives and social polarisation. Critics believe that campaigns against religious non-believers aim in part to deflect attention from regional governments' often egregious failures to curb corruption, protect democracy or improve development outcomes for the tens of millions of impoverished people in sub-Saharan African countries.

In 2025, religious non-believer communities in most sub-Saharan African countries have not generally found it possible to develop a viable resistance strategy to their stigmatisation. Some are in hiding and in fear of being attacked by mobs, encouraged by increased public stigmatisation of the community, sometimes led by the government. Stigmatisation of religious 'nones' – that is, people who lack belief in a religion – is likely when there is a decline in the quality of democracy. This has recently occurred in many African countries and as a result, religious non-believers' human rights have come under sustained attack. In short, religious nonbelievers in many sub-Saharan African countries, as well as nongovernmental advocacy organisations and individual activists advocating for the rights of nonbelievers, often face immense political, cultural, religious and social pressure.

The United States Commission on International Religious Freedom (USCIRF) released a 'factsheet' in 2021 highlighting the plight of the non-religious in Africa (USCIRF 2021). The examples described in the following paragraphs are extracted from the 2021 USCIRF 'factsheet'. The USCIRF report detailed incidents of arrests, detention, and imprisonment of religious nonbelievers, including those holding or advocating for the rights to hold non-religious beliefs. The 2021 USCIRF report provides examples from several sub-Saharan African countries, including Nigeria, Sudan, Uganda, Tanzania, South Africa and Kenya, which are briefly described in the following paragraphs in order to show the kind of stigmatisation and discrimination that the non-religious regularly face in some sub-Saharan African countries.

Mubarak Bala, president of the Nigerian Humanist Association, was arrested in April 2020 by Kano state, northern Nigeria, authorities. Mr Bala publicly declared his atheism in 2014 and from that time was a forthright advocate for Nigerian nonbelievers' rights. Mr Bala was arrested by Nigerian authorities and held without charge for several months. On 5 April 2022, he was sentenced to 24 years in prison at a (secular) high court in the northern state of Kano, pleading guilty to 24 charges relating to a Facebook post, one of which read: 'the fact is, you have no life after this one. You have been dead before, long before you were born, billions of years of death'. Mr Bal was also accused by lawyers in Kano state of posting items on Facebook that, they claimed, were 'insulting to Muslims'. State authorities restricted Mr Bala's access to his lawyer and for months refused to confirm his whereabouts and well-being, prior to the trial. Despite a federal court in Nigeria' capital, Abuja, ruling Mr Bala's detention unconstitutional and ordering him to be released, Kano state authorities refused and continued to incarcerate him when this chapter was written (October 2024).

Sudanese authorities arrested Mohamed Salih in May 2017 because he made a request to change the religious status on his national identification card from Muslim to non-religious. As a result, a judge declared him mentally 'disturbed' and 'unfit' to stand trial. Prior to the Sudanese revolution in April 2019, the government had applied a strict interpretation of Sunni Islam both to Muslims and non-Muslims. The country had draconian apostasy and blasphemy laws to try to prevent conversion from Islam to any other faith or non-belief, as with Mohamed Salih. Although in 2020 Sudan repealed this law, the country still faces challenges to ensure full religious freedom, including liberty not to follow a religious tradition.

Two leaders of Uganda's Humanist Association for Leadership Equality and Accountability (HALEA) were physically attacked in 2020. In addition, the HALEA offices were vandalised following the organisation's public promotion of freedom of thought and belief. No one was arrested for these crimes. In the same year, Tanzania's government failed to protect Ms Zara Kay, activist and founder of an Islamic feminist group, Faithless Hijabis, following accusations of advocating for apostasy and blasphemy in the country's capital, Dar es-Salaam. Members of Zara Kay's community declared that she was an apostate (in Arabic, *murtad*) – that is, a Muslim who has abandoned Islam in thought, word or deed – and she also received threats. When Ms Kay's case was reported to authorities, the government declined to take measures to protect her.

The cases of discrimination briefly described above, from Nigeria, Sudan, Uganda and Tanzania, illustrate that both individuals and representative organisations are under threat in various sub-Saharan African countries for publicly expressing non-religious views. This is not, however, the sum total of discrimination, as it also extends in some countries to schools and education, as well as employment.

In both South Africa and Uganda, some schools require all students, including nonbelievers, to partake in religious teaching, abide by religious rules and participate in rituals against their will, violating their rights not to participate in such activities. In Uganda, public schools are required by law to teach Islam or Christianity or both religions at the primary level. Non-religious students have no choice but to take part in these religious teachings. In Kenya, Mr Harrison Mumai, president of Atheists in Kenya Society, claimed that 'my public atheism made it more difficult for me to secure employment'. This claim followed his dismissal from the Kenyan Central Bank. Mr Mumai then claimed to have been interviewed for over 200 jobs but is not managed to secure employment. The reason, he claimed, was that putative employers informed him that they would not give him a job as they were concerned that his public atheism would deleteriously affect their businesses.

Collectively, these brief case studies illustrate how religious nones are discriminated against in some African countries. They also indicate that activists and organisations advocating on their behalf, face massive challenges to their ability to express their views publicly and to living according to their beliefs. In several regional countries, the non-religious face significant discrimination and stigmatisation in relation to education and employment, including both public and private sectors. Typically, governments fail to protect the non-religious from societal harassment and threats because they fear a societal backlash if they do: it is easier to 'go with the flow' and join in the persecution rather than take a principled stand. The consequence of government inaction is that the non-religious endure constant fear from discrimination, stigmatisation and harassment from self-proclaimed religious believers.

To improve the situation of religious nonbelievers in Africa, urgent steps should be taken, nationally and internationally, to address discrimination against and stigmatisation of the non-religious. The aim should be to encourage state neutrality in regards to matters of religion and, where constitutionally relevant, protect as country's secular status. Often, the non-religious are discriminated against and stigmatised because of a lack of government commitment to protect them; state and nonstate agencies undertaking such actions are not penalised, even when they clearly violate the rights of the non-religious (Humanists International 2021).

International human rights law makes it clear that no one who holds nonreligious and nontheistic beliefs should be killed or imprisoned. In addition, no one should be penalised for renouncing or criticising a religion, that is, declared an apostate and suffering the consequences, including persecution and in a small number of cases the murder of nonbelievers.

CONCLUSION

The issues of religious freedom and discrimination have increased in topicality and controversy in recent years, both within countries and internationally. The chapter surveyed state approaches to these issues. We saw that in some parts of the world; for example, some countries in the MENA and in sub-Saharan African states discriminate against religious minorities or the non-religious (also known as religious 'nones').

The chapter surveyed several topics under the general rubric of religious freedom and discrimination. We looked at state policies with respect to FoRB, with the USA as our main example. We also surveyed how the issue of international religious freedom became a key issue in international politics in the decades after World War II, stimulated by the Cold War involving the USA and the Soviet Union. Finally, the chapter examined three controversial topics in relation to religious freedom and discrimination: discrimination against religious minorities in the MENA, international religious discrimination against women and sexual minorities at the UN and discrimination against the non-religious in some sub-Saharan African countries.

QUESTIONS

1. Why do some states discriminate against some religious minorities?
2. Why did international religious freedom become a key focus of US foreign policy?
3. Why does a country with a secular constitution, such as Ghana, provide opportunities for religion to have a national policy role?
4. What are 'religious nones' and why do some states discriminate against such people?
5. Why does the UN, a secular organisation, allow religious conservatives to organise in support of 'family values'?

NOTE

1 IRFA aims 'To condemn violations of religious freedom, and to promote, and to assist other governments in the promotion of, the fundamental right to freedom of religion.' https://uscode.house.gov/view.xhtml?path=/prelim@title22/chapter73&edition=prelim

RECOMMENDED READINGS

Jonathan Fox, *Thou Shalt Have No Other Gods before Me: Why Governments Discriminate against Religious Minorities*, Cambridge: Cambridge University Press, 2020. Fox's book is a comprehensive analysis of the causes of religious discrimination, complete with detailed illustrations and anecdotes. Fox examines the causes of government-based religious discrimination against 771 minorities in 183 countries over the last quarter century. He also offers possible reasons why some minorities are discriminated against more than others, linking this to secular ideologies, religious monopolies, anti-cult policies and security concerns.

Luca Paladini, and Maria del Angel Iglesias Vazquez (eds.), *Promotion of Freedom of Religions and Beliefs in the European Context*, London: Springer, 2024. This book offers an in-depth analysis of a fundamental human freedom and a cornerstone of democracy: the Freedom of Religions or Beliefs (FoRB). The book focuses on the legal protection and promotion of FoRB in Europe because, in this context, exercising this right goes beyond a mere internal positioning in terms of legislation; rather, it is influenced by international and supranational case law, as well as the promotional activities of selected non-state subjects of international law.

Lina Papadopoulou, and Mark Hill (eds.), *Islam, Religious Liberty, and Constitutionalism in Europe*, London: Hart Publishing, 2024. This edited collection examines the tensions between Islam and European constitutionalism, focusing on constitutional challenges, religious freedom and other human rights, supranational and comparative approaches; and securitisation and Islamophobia.

ONLINE RESOURCES

International standards. UN Special Rapporteur on freedom of religion or belief. www.ohchr.org/en/special-procedures/sr-religion-or-belief/international-standards

Stop Hate UK. 'About Hate Crime. Religious Discrimination'. www.stophateuk.org/about-hate-crime/religious-discrimination/

The United States Commission on International Religious Freedom. www.uscirf.gov/

REFERENCES

Antisemitism in the Middle East: Unpacking the Root Causes and Implications for Regional Stability. 2023. 'Program on Extremism at the George Washington University'. https://extremism.gwu.edu/antisemitism-middle-east

Bettiza, Gregorio. 2019. *Finding Faith in Foreign Policy. Religion & American Diplomacy in a Postmodern World*. Oxford: Oxford University Press.

Bob, Clifford. 2019. 'Why Trump's new commission on unalienable rights is likely to upset the human rights community'. 'The Monkey Cage', *The Washington Post*, June 6.

Brammer, John Paul. 2018. 'Mike Pompeo still opposes gay marriage. Now he's about to be Secretary of State', *NBC News*. April 12. Accessed 23 June 2020. www.nbcnews.com/feature/nbc-out/mike-pompeo-still-opposes-gay-marriage-now-he-s-about-n865556

Casey, Shaun. 2017. 'How the state department has sidelined religion's role in diplomacy', *Religion & Politics*. September 5. Accessed 23 June 2020. https://religionandpolitics.org/2017/09/05/how-the-state-department-has-sidelined-religions-role-in-diplomacy/

Casey, Shaun. 2020. 'The gap between Trump's record and rhetoric on religious freedom', *Sojourners*. June 15. Accessed 24 June 2020. https://sojo.net/articles/gap-between-trumps-record-and-rhetoric-religious-freedom

Cesari, Jocelyne. 2021. *We God's People: Christianity, Islam and Hinduism in the World of Nations*. Cambridge: Cambridge University Press.

Ford, Liz. 2019. 'US accused of trying to dilute global agreements on women's rights', *The Guardian*. March 18. Accessed 23 June 2020. www.theguardian.com/global-development/2019/mar/18/us-accused-of-trying-to-dilute-international-agreements-un-commission-status-of-women

Fox, Jonathan. 2020. *Thou Shalt Have No Other Gods Before Me: Why Governments Discriminate against Religious Minorities*. Cambridge: Cambridge University Press.

Fox, Jonathan, and Lev Torpor. 2021. *Why Do People Discriminate Against Jews?* New York: Oxford University Press Academic.

FP Editors. 2019. 'What Trump promised Duda.' June 13. Accessed 23 June 2020. https://foreignpolicy.com/2019/06/13/what-trump-promised-duda/

Gevisser, Mark. 2020. *The Pink Line: The World's Queer Frontiers*. London: Profile Books.

Ghanea, Nazila. 2008. 'Religious or minority? Examining the realisation of international standards in relation to religious minorities in the Middle East', *Religion, State & Society*, 36, 3: 303–25.

Glendon, Mary Ann (2010) "God and Mrs Roosevelt", *First Things*, May. www.firstthings.com/article/2010/05/god-and-mrs-roosevelt

Hannum, Hurst. 2018. 'Minority rights', *Oxford Bibliographies*. Accessed 11 November 2022. www.oxfordbibliographies.com/view/document/obo-9780199743292/obo-9780199743292-0120.xml

Haynes, Jeffrey. 2008. 'Religion and a human rights culture in America'. *The Review of Faith & International Affairs*, 6: 73–82.

Haynes, Jeffrey. 2013. 'The "Arab Uprising", Islamists and democratization', in Jeffrey Haynes and Guy Ben-Porat (eds.), '*Religion, Secularism and Politics: A Mediterranean View*', special issue of *Mediterranean Politics*, 18, 2: 170–188.

Haynes, Jeffrey. 2014. *Faith-Based Organizations at the United Nations*. New York: Palgrave Macmillan.

Haynes, Jeffrey. 2019. *From Huntington to Trump. Thirty Years of the Clash of Civilizations*. Lanham/Boulder/New York/London: Lexington Books.

Haynes, Jeffrey. 2020. 'Trump and the politics of international religious freedom', *Religions*, 11 (8), 385. https://doi.org/10.3390/rel11080385

Haynes, Jeffrey, Peter Hough, and Bruce Pilbeam. 2023. *World Politics: International Relations and Globalisation in the 21st Century*, 3rd ed. London: Sage.

Humanists International. 2021. *New Report Sheds Light on Persecution of Non-believers in Africa*. https://humanists.international/blog/new-report-sheds-light-on-persecution-of-non-believers-in-africa/

Mbiti, John S. 1975. *Introduction to African Religion*. London: Heinemann. https://scielo.org.za/scielo.php?script=sci_arttext&pid=S2413-9467201 9000300021

Minority Rights. 2010. *Minority Rights: International Standards and Guidance for Implementation*. New York and Geneva: United Nations Human Rights. Accessed 11 November 2022. www.ohchr.org/sites/default/files/Documents/Publications/MinorityRights_en.pdf

Mundy, Jacob. 2010. 'The failure of minority transformative politics in Algeria: The Kabilyi citizens' movement and the state', in Michael U. Mbasano and Chima J. Korieh (eds.), *Minorities and the State in Africa*. Amherst: Cambria Press.

Petersen, Marie Juul. 2021. 'The International Promotion of Freedom of Religion or Belief: Key Debates and Divides', in Jeffrey Haynes (ed.), *Handbook on Religion and International Relations*, Cheltenham: Edward Elgar, 215–30.

Quashigah, Kofi. 2010. 'Religion and the secular state in Ghana', *Religion and the Secular State: National Reports under the direction of Javier Martinez-Torrónand W. Cole Durham, Jr.*' Provo, UT: The International Center for Law and Religion Studies, Brigham Young University.

Stewart, Katherine. 2020. *The Power Worshippers: Inside the Dangerous Rise of Religious Nationalism*. London: Bloomsbury.

Tóibín, Colm. 2020. Review of Mark Gevisser's The Pink Line', *The Guardian*. June 20. Accessed 24 June 2020. www.theguardian.com/books/2020/jun/20/the-pink-line-by-mark-gevisser-review-the-worlds-queer-frontiers

The United States Commission on International Religious Freedom. 2021. *Factsheet. The Condition of Nonbelievers in Africa*. www.uscirf.gov/sites/default/files/2021-07/2021%20Factsheet%20-%20Nonbelievers.pdf

Verma, Pranshu. 2020. 'Pompeo's human rights panel could hurt L.G.B.T. and women's rights, critics say'. *The New York Times*, June 23.

NATION AND NATIONALISM

SECULAR NATIONALISM

Our discussion commences with a discussion of secular nationalism, in order to locate the issue of religious nationalism in an appropriate intellectual and ideological context. Overall, the aim of the chapter is to illustrate how religion often has a significant role in relation to the nation and nationalism in today's world.

It is now widely recognised that religious affiliation and nationalism — that is, identification with one's own nation and support for its interests, especially to the exclusion or detriment of the interests of other nations — are often closely connected. As two kinds of self-identification, while sometimes in tension, often they are not; either coexisting unproblematically, or acting in mutually supportive ways. Various approaches are suggested to explain the relationship between religious affiliation and nationalism. Rather than 'either or', the relationship between nationalism and religion should be seen as a continuum. At one end is an ideal-type 'secular nationalism', and at the other, there is 'religious nationalism'. Somewhere in the middle is 'civil-religious nationalism', for decades believed to be the situation in various countries, notably the USA, with characteristics of both.

DOI: 10.4324/9781003508823-7

> **INTRODUCTORY BOX : SECULAR NATIONALISM**
>
> The term 'secular nationalism' – which I shall refer to in this chapter simply as nationalism in order to differentiate between it and religious nationalism – is both dogma – that is, a set of views – and political movement, that is, political activity in pursuit of a particular goal. The concept of nationalism emphasises that a nation – conventionally understood as a group of people of indeterminate but normally considerable size often in the context of a country, who believe themselves linked by significant community ties – has the political right to constitute itself as an independent, sovereign political community, both because of a shared history and a perceived common destiny. For nationalists, it is only right and proper that state borders should dovetail, as precisely as possible, with the boundaries of the nation. In extreme cases, such as that demonstrated in the ideology of Nazi Germany, the state regards the nation as *the* supreme facet of a person's identity, which can override all other relevant concerns, such as religion, class or race.

Many, but by no means all, nationalists are politically conservative, with views which may accord both with right-wing populism and an anti-immigration stance. As we saw in Chapter 4, right-wing populists in several Western nations have recently either won power or achieved a significantly increased share of the vote without gaining control, including in the USA, Australia, India and numerous European countries, among them the Czech Republic, Denmark, France, Germany, Hungary, Italy, the Netherlands, Poland, Slovakia and Sweden (Haynes 2019).

In this regard, the 2017–21 Donald Trump administration in the USA has attracted much attention from political scientists, including those with an interest in relationships between religion and politics. Trump's election as US president in November 2016 both symbolised and manifested a more general international rise of populist nationalism with religious connotations. Achieving power with the invaluable assistance of the votes of white Christian conservatives, Trump made plain his anti-immigrant, especially anti-Mexican and anti-Muslim, views. He swiftly introduced a policy to prevent Muslims from named countries entering the

USA and promised to build a 'big, beautiful' wall to keep out 'Mexicans', identified by Trump as rapists and criminals (Haynes 2019). During the 2016 presidential election campaign, the issue of immigration was central to political debates between presidential candidates. The focus, on the one hand, was on illegal immigration into the USA from Mexico and Central America and, on the other hand, there was the question of some immigrants' loyalty to the USA. Trump and several other Republican candidates openly questioned the loyalties of American Muslims, of which there are more than three million in the USA. Both issues centre on whether specific groups of people – that is, 'Mexicans' and Muslims – are to be fully trusted by Americans. Do they demonstrate 'sufficient' and 'acceptable' levels of nationalist loyalty, commitment and identity to the USA?

BOX 7.1 CAN IMMIGRANTS AND FOREIGNERS BE TRUSTED?

The issue of whether immigrants and foreigners can be trusted was raised by Donald Trump during and after his successful electoral campaign in 2016. Trump was not the only nationalist to raise this issue. Another was Trump's friend and ally, Hungary's prime minister, Viktor Orbán, another right-wing nationalist. Both Trump and Orbán refer to 'the people' in a specific way and with a certain understanding of what the term implies: They do not mean *all* their country's citizens. They are referring to those they see as 'our' people, that is, certain groups: white-skinned Christians, not 'swarthy' Latinos or religiously beyond-the-pale Muslims.

The Italian political scientist, Raffaele Marchetti refers to this linking of culture and religion with nationalism as 'civil sationism'. Marchetti explains that 'the civilizational model is centred on the primacy of the cultural and religious bond' within the political and economic context of globalisation, characterised by a high degree of political and economic exclusion of certain groups of people. According to Marchetti, 'the perspective of civilizations offers grounds for a conservative rejection of global transformations' with 'key factors contributing to conflict principally relate to the fact of irreducible cultural differences' (Marchetti 2016: 122–3).

'Irreducible cultural differences' are, they claim, what principally animates right-wing nationalists in, *inter alia*: the USA, Russia, India, Myanmar, Australia, Canada and numerous European countries. In these countries, Muslims are usually the 'Other', who right-wing nationalists target with abuse and condemnation. It is not however especially important if there are really 'irreducible cultural differences' between the Indigenous population and non-Indigenous Muslim communities. The key issue is instead a political consideration: Can the nationalist politician persuade sufficient voters that such differences exist and that they are so important that they will cast their ballots for them? Buzan and Waever (2009) remind us that 'limited collectivities (states, nations, and as anticipated by Huntington, civilisations) engage in self-reinforcing rivalries with other limited collectivities and ... such interaction strengthens their we-feeling'. Because this 'involves a reference to a "we", it is a social construct operative in the interaction among people. A main criterion of this type of referent is that it forms an interpretative community: that it is the context in which principles of legitimacy and valuation circulate and within which the individual constructs an interpretation of events' (Buzan and Waever 2009: 255). In other words, vote for me and I'll save you from the bad guys. Who are the bad guys? Anyone sufficiently different from 'us' to warrant the term and thus warrant our suspicion.

The global transformations that Marchetti (2016) refers to in Box 7.1 are multifaceted. They involve momentous political, social, economic and technological changes which have taken place since the end of the Cold War in the late 1980s. An important manifestation of these changes is an increasing focus on identity, involving various religious and cultural – that is, 'civilisational' – configurations. In the early 1990s, political globalisation, following pressure from the governments of the USA and various European countries, including the United Kingdom, France and Germany, focused on efforts to bring about widespread liberal democracy and improved human rights, including greater religious freedom. Today, however, we see widespread derailing of such liberal values, with widespread democratic 'backsliding' and pervasive attacks on human rights, including religious freedom.

In the mid-2020s, right-wing nationalists were riding the crest of the wave of these developments; many were benefitting electorally. According to the American sociologist, Rogers Brubaker (2017), right-wing nationalists benefit electorally from 'two sets of decades-spanning structural trends', which involve four 'transformations': 'party politics, social structure, media, and governance structures'. According to Brubaker, they promote 'a generic populism – a heightened tendency to address "the people" directly – and the demographic, economic, and cultural transformations that have encouraged more specific forms of protectionist populism'. Brubaker identifies these changes as occurring from the mid-2000s, linked to a 'conjunctural coming-together of a series of [security] crises': 'the security crisis', consequential to a succession of terror attacks by Islamist extremists since 9/11, 'the Great Recession and sovereign debt crisis' in 2008, and 'the refugee crisis' of 2015, stemming from Syria's tragic civil war. They occurred 'in the context of a crisis of public knowledge – to form a "perfect storm" that was powerfully conducive to populist claims to protect the people against threats to their economic, cultural, and physical security' (Brubaker 2017: 369).

The conditions that Brubaker (2017) describes are the backdrop for the political efflorescence of right-wing nationalists and their electorally effective references to alleged cultural and religious differences in many countries around the world.

NATIONALISM AND RELIGION

The relationship between religion and nationalism is not self-evident. Many acclaimed writers on nationalism, including the British-Czech philosopher and social anthropologist, Ernest Gellner (1983), and the British historian, Eric Hobsbawm (1990) do not include religion in their analyses of nationalism. Gellner and Hobsbawm highlight in their analyses the significance of various secular historical and economic factors in the development of nationalism over time. Today, however, it is widely recognised that to arrive at a comprehensive understanding of the development of nationalism in the modern world, we need to consider both the direct and indirect influence of religion in order fully to comprehend the current manifestations of nationalism.

The British historical sociologist, Anthony D. Smith, is a key authority on religious nationalism. Discussing the relationship between religion and nationalism, Smith (2003: ix) claims that 'perhaps more detrimental than anything to our understanding of these phenomena has been the general trend to dismiss the role of religion and tradition in a globalizing world, and to downplay the persistence of nationalism in a "post-national" global order'. Smith's 2003 book, *Chosen Peoples: Sacred Sources of National Identity*, argues that the relationship between religion and nationalism is highly important. For Smith, 'even' secular nationalism, often thought of as an archetypally irreligious ideology, typically draws on religious understandings of the world. In support of Smith's claim, it will be very difficult to understand American nationalism both historically and today without considering formative Christian – actually, mainline Protestant – beliefs and values (Green, Rozell, and Wilcox 2003).

When the relationship between religion and nationalism is clear and sustained, then we employ a hybrid term: 'religious nationalism'. Religious nationalism signifies a demonstrably close, even synonymous, relationship between two concepts 'religion' and 'nationalism', which are not necessarily ideologically close. Religion fits in in this context when it is a defining component of what a nation is said to comprise, helping to forge a collective ethos of identity and belonging expressed in a collective culture. Religious nationalism's ideological importance is clear in various political and cultural contexts. For example, when the state, as in Iran or Saudi Arabia, or in Afghanistan under the Taliban (1996–2001, from 2021), claims to derive its political legitimacy from popular adherence to religious not secular doctrines, then Western political science calls it a theocracy. This derives from the belief that the state's ideology is dominated by religious values, beliefs and ideals.

Note, however, that simply to point to potential relationships between the concepts of 'religion' and 'nationalism' as autonomous entities that may sometimes amalgamate is not sufficient to comprehend the fact that the relationship between religion and nationalism has long been understood as a fundamental component of the nation. The French aristocrat, diplomat, sociologist, political scientist, political philosopher and historian, Alexis de Tocqueville's 1835 book, *Democracy in America*, contended that religion was one of three basic elements that provided a nation with its contract. In *The Elementary Forms of Religious Life* (1912), the French sociologist, Emile Durkheim, argued that in Western modernity, new forms of expression of the sacred emerge that compete with established religious sects, such as Christianity. This might be the nation that makes sacred cultural or patriotic bonds believed to unite the entire national community. Alternatively, it might be humans who seek to make sacred concepts such as individual human rights a pivotal component of modern democratic political systems. Finally, in *Essays on the Sociology of Religion*, the German sociologist, Max Weber, examined the differentiation between religious, political and cultural spheres so as to contextualise relationships between religion and politics.

Religious nationalism is not solely a modern phenomenon, as it has also appeared historically. For example, it was a pivotal ideology in relation to events in the early twentieth century. This was the time of nationalism's burgeoning in anticolonial struggles in many parts of then-colonised areas of the world, including sub-Saharan Africa, Asia, and the Middle East and North Africa. During control of much of the global south, Western powers sought to develop modern secular regimes, which, however, frequently had an unintended outcome: anticolonial, indigenous, religion and culture-inspired, opposition movements. In the decades before and after World War I (1914–18), many colonies in the global south underwent significant political upheavals, within which various religious expressions – including, Hinduism, Buddhism and Islam – dovetailed with expressions of secular nationalism, to produce a hybrid ideology: religious nationalism, which characterised most expressions of anti-colonial opposition. As a result, Pakistan was explicitly founded as a Muslim state in 1947, religiously and culturally distinct from Hindu-dominated India, following the withdrawal of British colonial rule. Buddhism was of great political importance in various Southeast and East Asian countries, including Burma/Myanmar and Vietnam, in the context of their struggle for liberation from, respectively, British and French colonial rule. After World War I, the rise of nationalism in the Middle East and North Africa was strongly associated with Islam – both as religion and culture – which coalesced as the key component of militant, anti-colonial ideology demanding renewal and reassertion of national, religious and cultural identities (Haynes, Hough and Pilbeam 2023).

Following the long wave of decolonisation in the global south which started around the time of World War I and ended more than half a century later, David Little, Emeritus Professor of the Practice in Religion, Ethnicity and International Conflict, asserted in the early 1990s, that many post-colonial nation-building projects were 'deeply infused with religion':

> Whether the issue is building, restructuring or maintaining a nation, the process is, all over the world, deeply infused with religion. How else are we to understand Northern Ireland, Israel, Lebanon, the Sudan, Sri Lanka, or Iran? Or, more immediately, how else are we to understand former Eastern European satellites like Poland or Bulgaria, or the so-called 'Soviet Nationalities,' such as the Ukraine, Lithuania, or Azerbaijan and Armenia? Nor, for that matter, are the developed countries altogether exempt from the effects of religious nationalism. The influence of the Moral Majority [that is, the Christian Right] and related movements on American public life during the 1980s left no doubt about that.
>
> (Little 1994: 84)

When Little wrote these words, novel expressions of 'religious nationalism' were becoming apparent in, for example, former Yugoslavia, consequential to the end of the Cold War, the collapse of the Soviet Union and multifaceted impacts of globalisation.

BOX 7.2 BUDDHIST NATIONALISM AND CONFLICT IN SRI LANKA

The widespread reappearance of nationalism has attracted the attention of both scholars and policymakers. Across the world, it seems, from the Philippines and India to the United States and Brazil, nationalism is helping shape government policies. We have already noted the Hindu nationalist policies of Narendra Modi and the Bharatiya Janata Party (BJP) in India. In addition to India, another South Asian country, Sri Lanka, is also an example of the political impact of religious nationalism. Although Buddhist nationalism is a defining force in Sri Lanka, its development has received much less attention than Hindu nationalism in India, no doubt because India is both the regional giant and a possessor of nuclear weapons which India has highlighted in its long-running dispute with Muslim-majority, Pakistan.

Buddhist nationalism in Sri Lanka is closely associated with a group of radical Buddhist monks, known as the Bodu Bala Sena (BBS), with close links to the country's long-established Rajapaksa political dynasty. Since the late 2000s, the BBS and the Rajapaksas have worked to integrate Buddhist nationalism into Sri Lanka's political framework. Over time, Buddhist nationalism has played a significant role in Sri Lanka's domestic and foreign policies. A downside is that Buddhist nationalism marginalises Sri Lankans from minority communities, while threatening to create a new era of conflict, following Sri Lanka's civil war, from 1983 until 2009.

While Buddhism is commonly associated with both non-violence and peace, Buddhist nationalism does not conform to this conventional wisdom. In Sri Lanka, Buddhism is politicised, often merging with political parties' ideological visions. The BBS is an important component of this situation, able consistently to influence political leaders and their policies. For example, when Gotabaya Rajapaksa, president of Sri Lanka between 2019 and 2022, and then-defence minister, visited a new Buddhist brigade school in 2014, he stated the following: 'It is the monks who protect our country, religion and race' (*BBC News* 2023). Such a statement, coming just five years after the end of a decades-long civil war fought along ethnic-religious lines between Buddhist Sinhalese and Hindu Tamils, did nothing to promote national unity. Instead, Rajapaksa's statement appeared to demonstrate his vision of Sri Lanka as a Sinhalese Buddhist country (Malji 2021).

NATIONALISM AND CONFUCIANISM

Confucianism is an ancient religious and philosophical system. It has developed over the last 2,500 years from writings attributed to a Chinese philosopher, Confucius (the latinised version of Kung Fu-tzu (that is, Master Kung), a teacher in China who lived between *c.* 551 and 479 BCE). His key teachings were concerned with principles of good conduct, practical wisdom and 'proper' social relationships and focused upon relationships between individuals, between individuals and their families, and between individuals and general society.

The German sociologist Max Weber (1969: 21) noted that, in China, Confucianism was historically 'the status ethic of prebendaries, of men with literary educations who were characterized by a secular rationalism'. This underlines how important it was in China to belong to the *cultured* stratum; if one did not, he (much less she) did not count; and an adhesion to Confucian values was an important element. As a result, Confucianism was a status ethic of the 'cultured' stratum that in turn not only helped determine the way of life in China itself but also influenced neighbouring areas that historically came under Chinese influence or control, including present-day Korea, Japan, Singapore, Taiwan and Vietnam. In Korea, for example, Confucianism grew in significance from the seventh century CE to become not only the traditional ideological core of the governing system but also a religious or philosophical system which affected the social and cultural aspects of the nation's life (Barr 2023).

Over time, countries influenced by Confucianism diverged politically. On the one hand, China, North Korea and Vietnam are three of the few remaining communist countries. On the other hand, from the time of the Cold War, which began in the late 1940s and ended 40 years later, Japan, South Korea, Singapore and Taiwan were closely allied with the USA and more generally the West. This suggests that while these countries may share cultural characteristics that highlight the importance of the community or the collective over the individual, a shared background in Confucianism does not dictate similar political developments or international relations.

In China, Confucian cultural and religious factors can be seen today in relation to a 'post-communist' ideology that emphasises certain patterns of living and standards of social value, while also providing an important backdrop to recent developments in political thinking and foreign policy, including in relation to Chinese nationalism (Barr 2023).

A leading Chinese intellectual, Jiang Qing, argues that the 'Confucian religion is the core of Chinese civilization, including political, cultural and religious aspects'. Confucianism is in practice China's state religion. Jian Qing argues that Confucianism is both 'cultural consensus' and 'the spiritual belief of the whole nation' ('Confucianism will never be religion' 2006). For Jiang Qing, government is legitimate only when it clearly reflects the values associated with the community's cultural traditions and principles and in China, he contends, this is Confucianism. Chinese nationalism informed by Confucianism underlines for the Chinese government the inappropriateness of Western-style, political and social values. Instead, under the leadership of the Chinese communist party, China's national political institutions and practices seek reflect local cultural values, highlighting the continuing ideological relevance of Confucianism ('Confucianism will never be religion' 2006). Critics contend, however, that China's Confucian-inspired nationalism 'negate[s] the generalisation of Western principles like democracy, freedom, and human rights etc.' (Ommerborn 2003).

NATIONALISM AND CHRISTIANITY

The phenomenon of Christian nationalism is strongly linked to the recent presidency of Donald Trump (2017–21) in the USA. Whitehead and Perry argue that Christian nationalism in the USA fuses multiple markers of traditional American identity (including, Christianity, whiteness, normative political and social conservatism) into a single cultural framework that, while not limited to devout Christian evangelicals, is strongly associated with them (Whitehead and Perry 2020).

Between one-third and three quarters of Americans consider that religion is losing influence in their society. Despite this, religion continues to manifest institutional strength in the USA. This is reflected both in comparatively high numbers of self-proclaimed believers and regular attendance at religious services as well as in numerous religious entities regularly engaging in public debates, discussion and lobbying. This questions the idea of a declining *public* role for religion, even when for many Americans religious faith is an increasingly *private* matter. A more individualistic religious perspective is now common among Americans, including the rapid growth of 'religious nones' who now comprise a quarter of adult Americans, making 'no religious belief' the second largest group in the USA. In this sense, religion is rapidly declining, a result of changing values – informed by personal and group decisions. As religion loses its grip on the minds and thought processes of many Americans, especially the young, it signifies a cleavage between declining numbers of Americans who believe that the USA was and should remain a 'Christian nation' and those Americans who believe strongly in religious pluralism, without a predominant role for traditional Christian beliefs. This does not represent a clear change in the form of linkage between religion and politics: it is not desacralisation of the mass political realm, which the secularisation thesis claimed would happen consequent to modernisation. Today's America is religiously contoured by both fragmentation and voluntarism, shaping how religion intersects with mass political and social life.

During the Trump presidency, religion's public political role was a key factor in America's long-running culture wars. The key issue is: what *should* religious actors be allowed to contribute to political life in the USA, given the constitutional constraints on links between religion and politics in that country? Some contend that the language of the First Amendment of the US Constitution – that is, 'Congress shall make no law respecting an establishment of religion or prohibiting the free exercise thereof' – significantly restricts religion's ability to engage in politics, *de facto* condemning them to separate realms and forever dividing them. Others argue that the First Amendment is primarily about protecting religion from the state, implying that it is entirely appropriate that religion has public religious views and roles. This argument – that is, over the allowable limits of 'religious expression by public authority'

(Wald 1991: 238) – is the substance of the culture wars. As already noted, the controversy is not new: the US political system has long provided a fertile environment for the expression of religious differences in the public realm. What is different today is that the controversy extends to a new and contentious ideology: Christian nationalism.

Constitutionally, the USA is a secular state, that is, the governmental apparatus is formally independent of religion. Nevertheless, religious issues are often of great important to politics. Although 65% of Americans state that they are Christian (Pew Research Center 2019), churches do not enjoy a favoured constitutional role; the rights of citizenship are not reserved only for Christians; and secular, not religious law, formally regulates citizens' conduct. Yet, secularisation is not *only* about a formal divorce of church and state; in European secular societies, for example, those in France, the United Kingdom and Sweden, public attitudes to religion range from indifference to outspoken hostility (Kuenkler, Madeley and Shankar 2019). Today, the USA, like other Western countries, is an increasingly secular society (Pew Research Center 2019). Christian nationalism, which emerged, or perhaps better to say became politically significant during the Trump presidency, informed President Trump's brand of culture wars-themed politics. Many Christian nationalists in the USA want to reverse secularisation via legislation, not by 'mere' exhortations to Christian morality.

Today's Christian nationalists have their roots in earlier religiously informed conservative movements, such as Jerry Falwell's 'Moral Majority', known variously as the Religious Right or Christian Right, formed in 1979. Christian nationalists claim to be defending 'Christian values' against the onslaught of secularisation, seeking to reverse secularisation and liberalism, including legal abortion, absence or downgrading of prayers in state-run schools and science teaching that adopts a rationalist, rather than a 'Creationist', perspective. Until the presidency of Donald Trump, the achievements of Christian nationalists, of which there were only a relatively few, were modest. The issues on which Christian nationalists mainly focus – that is, abortion, sexuality and attempts to defend religion (as in the case of 'creation science') against the claims of science – are regarded by many Americans as matters of personal preference not political diktat (Pew Research Center 2019).

> **BOX 7.3 CHRISTIAN NATIONALISM IN WEST AFRICA: THE CASE OF GHANA**
>
> Christian nationalism is a modern form of religious nationalism, drawing on specific Christian values and beliefs. Christian nationalism is understood in various ways. Some contend that Christian nationalism is a healthy form of Christian patriotism, of loving God and loving one's country. Others understand Christian nationalism as a religious and political project to make publicly dominant a singular interpretation of Christianity. In the United States, a recent scholarly focus on Christian nationalism, Whitehead and Perry (2020: 10) define Christian nationalism as 'a collection of myths, traditions, symbols, narratives, and value systems that idealizes and advocates a fusion of Christianity with American civic life'. They argue that in the USA, Christian nationalism is undergirded by identification with a conservative political orientation (though not necessarily a political party), Bible belief, premillennial visions of moral decay and divine sanction for conquest.
>
> This characterisation of Christian nationalism is relevant to Ghana, as Christian nationalists in that country advocate a fusion of Christianity with civic life. In addition, they adhere to traditional political values while not necessarily belonging to the same political party. Their ideas are typically expressed by quoting verses from the Bible, and they often allude to severe moral decline in Ghana. In Ghana, influential individual Christian nationalists, as well as prominent churches, such as Ghana's largest, the Church of Pentecost, seek to realise God's kingdom on earth via dominion theology (Haynes 2023).

NATIONALISM AND ISLAM

Many Islamists – that is, those who advocate increasing the influence of Islamic law in politics and society – would contend that

Islam as a religion somehow 'forbids' nationalism based on identity with an individual nation-state. This is because the *ummah* – that is, the whole community of Muslims, bound together by ties of religion – should, according to Islamists, be impervious to nationalist appeals. However, such an assertion is difficult to support for two main reasons: first, nationalism appears to be a very widespread, perhaps universal, phenomenon, whose adherents include many Muslims in numerous individual countries. Second, various Islamic textual sources make it clear that separate national loyalties are acceptable. For example, a verse in the Muslim holy book, the *Qur'an*, proclaims that God (Allah in Islamic terminology) has created different 'tribes and peoples, so that they should get to know each other' (Qur'an 49:13). In addition, there is a *hadith* – that is, a saying of the Prophet Mohammed – stating that 'Love of your homeland is part of your faith' (quoted in Mandi 2006: 10).

There are around 50 countries in the world with Muslim-majority populations. Many among them have strongly nationalist and patriotic sentiments, often encouraged by governments, and sometimes directed against fellow Muslim peoples (e.g. Iranians/Iraqis, especially during their 1980–88 war; Sudanese/Egyptians at various times and Uzbeks/Tajiks in Afghanistan). This adherence to national as opposed to Islamic identities is reflected in the way that some governments in Muslim-majority countries in the Middle East and North Africa seek to invoke elements of their country's pre-Islamic historical pasts as a form of governmental legitimation, even though in each case the pre-Muslim past is officially one of *jahiliya* (ignorance). For example, Egypt commemorates the Pharaohs; Tunisia looks to the Phoenicians; Iran, especially under the pre-revolution shahs, highlights the ancient Persian empires; while Yemen lionises the ancient, pre-Islamic, kingdoms Saba and Himyar. These examples underline important aspects of contemporary nationalism in several Muslim-majority countries in the Middle East and North Africa, which are both earlier and separated from a shared Islamic heritage.

The rise of the modern state after World War I – with its rigorously defended borders, centralised political and administrative powers, and ubiquitous bureaucratic structures – was instrumental in diluting, rarely breaking, historically rooted networks built on communities of scholars and mystics and commerce. At the same time, we need to be aware of what is known as 'Islamic transnationalism', a phenomenon with both historical and doctrinal elements. Islamic transnationalism refers to cross-border activities of Islamic movements, such as the Muslim Brotherhood, al Qaeda and Islamic State. They operate for various purposes (including commercial, financial, political, religious and terroristic) and have long characterised the international politics of the Muslim world.

In terms of doctrine and political ideas, the *ummah* has been subject for more than a century to many, often competing, ideologies and doctrines that appeared in one country and then spread. For example, the modern religious ideology of Wahhabism, a puritanical interpretation of Islam which became a transnational ideology adhered to by, among others, al Qaeda and Islamic State, developed from the ideas of Mohammad ibn Abd-al-Wahhab, an eighteenth-century Arabian Sunni Muslim reformer. Wahhabism dynamically emerged from the Arabian Peninsula 200 years ago, taking root among Sunni Muslims in many parts of the Middle East and elsewhere.

Al-Wahhab believed that Islam had been corrupted more than a thousand years earlier, shortly after the death of the Prophet Muhammad. As a result, he denounced any theology – including religious scholarship – and customs that had since developed as 'non-Islamic'. In a religious revolution, he and his supporters took over what is now Saudi Arabia, where his ideology – known as Wahhabism – continues to be both the state ideology and the dominant school of religio-political thought.

Wahhabism has two central tenets: (1) preaching against worship of 'false idols', including a popular, mystical form of Islam known as Sufism. This is because followers of Sufism – known as, Sufis – worship local saints as well as God and (2) Sunni Wahhabists regard Shias as apostates, that is, religious non-believers. Shiism is a strand of Islam whose followers revere the descendants of Ali, the Prophet Mohammed's son-in-law.

Sayyid Qutb (1906–1966) was a more recent religious and ideological thinker who informed both al Qaeda and Islamic State's transnational ideology. Qutb was an Egyptian, a prominent Islamist and a member of the Muslim Brotherhood, the Arab world's oldest Islamist group, which advocates an Islamic state in Egypt. His thought was deeply influenced by the revolutionary radicalism of a contemporaneous Indian Islamist, Sayyid Abu'l-A'la Mawdudi (1903–1979). Qutb's ideological development fell into two distinct periods: before 1954, and from 1954 until his execution by the Egyptian government in 1966, following imprisonment and torture by the secularist government of Gamal Abdel Nasser. Following an attempt on Nasser's life in October 1954, the government imprisoned thousands of members of the Muslim Brotherhood, including Qutb, and officially banned the organisation. Qutb declared 'Western civilization' to be the enemy of Islam, denounced leaders of Muslim nations for not following Islam closely enough, and sought to spread the belief among Sunni Muslims that it was their duty to undertake jihad to defend and purify Islam (Hassan 2016).

Akbarzadeh and Connor (2005) note that nationalism has undermined all attempts at transnational unity within the Arab/Muslim world. This emphasises that over the last century the Muslim world has been emphatically divided into separate nations, largely the result of adhesion to imported, secular, Western notions of nationalism. The result is a paradox: on the one hand, all Muslims declare one faith and belief in one God, and in some important ways – for example, the *hajj* (pilgrimage) to Mecca and Medina – a shared sense of history and community – many feel connected by their faith as part of a transnational community. However, on the other hand, this does not by any means imply that this feeling of community inevitably surpasses other, more particularistic, including national, identities. This implies that most Muslims have no problem with having a number of identities, including national identity based on a secular ideology: nationalism.

CONCLUSION

The relationship between religion and nationalism is complex. It raises the issue of identity, posing the question: To whom or what does an individual owe his or her allegiance? Is it to one's faith or is it to one's nation and state? Secularisation, political scientists widely anticipated, would lead to the demise of religion and the dominance of secular nationalism, with the latter replacing religion in people's affections. This did not however happen or, to put it differently, it did not happen in a clear and continuous way. Instead, there was a coming together of apparently different sources of identity coexisting in many individuals, both religious and national, which many governments have sought to exploit for their own purposes.

QUESTIONS

1. What are the main differences between secular and religious nationalism?
2. Why do some scholars of nationalism ignore religion?
3. Why is the United States a country which has seen the growing political importance of Christian nationalism?
4. What is Islamic nationalism?
5. Identify and explain the links between Confucianism and nationalism in China.

RECOMMENDED READINGS

Koushiki Dasgupta, *Ascetics as Activists: Saffron Women of Hindu Nationalism*, London: Bloomsbury, 2025. Dasgupta examines the position of the female ascetics or sadhvis within the right-wing Hindu nationalist discourse in India.

Nora Fisher-Onar, *Contesting Pluralism(s): Islamism, Liberalism, and Nationalism in Turkey and Beyond*, Cambridge: Cambridge University Press, 2024. Beginning with the aftermath of the 2016 attempted coup in Turkey, Contesting Pluralism(s) challenges a widespread tendency to limit studies of Turkish-and Muslim-politics to 'Islamist vs. secularist' or 'Islam vs. democracy' debates.

Richard T. Hughes, and Christina Littlefield, *Christian America and the Kingdom of God: White Christian Nationalism from the Puritans through January 6, 2021*, Champaign, IL: University of Illinois Press, 2025. Richard T. Hughes and Christina Littlefield draw on discussions of civil religion and forms of nationalism to explore the complex legal and cultural arguments for a Christian America.

J. Christopher Soper, and Joel S. Fetzer, *Religion and Nationalism in Global Perspective*, Cambridge: Cambridge University Press, 2018. While the subject has received both scholarly and popular attention, this distinctive book is the first comparative study to examine the origins and development of three distinct models: religious nationalism, secular nationalism and civil-religious nationalism.

ONLINE RESOURCES

Boston University's Institute on Culture, Religion, and World Affairs (CURA). CURA brings together a multi-disciplinary community of scholars to encourage and support research on the role of religion in public affairs. Established in 1985, CURA is the oldest centre for the study of religion and world affairs in the United States. Supported by a substantial endowment and grants from funders such as the Henry Luce Foundation, the Templeton Foundation, the Bradley Foundation, the Kroc Institute for International Peace and the Metanexus Foundation, CURA has sponsored over 140 research projects on five continents that have led to the publication of over 145 books. www.bu.edu/cura/about-cura/

Pew Forum on Religion and Public Life. The Forum, launched in 2001, seeks to promote a deeper understanding of issues at the intersection of religion and public affairs. The Forum pursues its mission by delivering timely, impartial information to national opinion leaders, including government officials and journalists. As a nonpartisan, non-advocacy organisation, the Forum does not take positions on policy debates. www.pewforum.org/

REFERENCES

Akbarzadeh, Shahram, and Kylie Connor. 2005. 'The organization of the Islamic conference: Sharing an illusion', *Middle East Policy.* June 22. http://goliath.ecnext.com/coms2/gi_0199-4433863/The-Organization-of-the-Islamic.html

Barr, Michael. 2023. 'Confucianism: Classical, neo- and "new"', in Jeffrey Haynes (ed.), *The Routledge Handbook of Religion and Politics*, 3rd ed. London: Routledge, 66–80.

BBC News. 2023. 'The hardline Buddhists targeting Sri Lanka's Muslims', *BBC News*. www.bbc.co.uk/news/world-asia-21840600

Brubaker, Rogers. 2017. Why populism'?, *Theory and Society*, 5: 357–85.

Buzan, Barry, and Ole Waever. 2009. 'Macrosecuritisation and security constellations: Reconsidering scale in securitisation theory', *Review of International Studies,* 35: 253–76.

'Confucianism will never be religion'. 2006. *China Daily,* 6 January. www.chinadaily.com.cn/english/doc/2006-01/06/content_509753.htm

Gellner, Ernest. 1983. *Nations and Nationalism.* Ithaca: Cornell University Press.

Green, John C., Mark J. Rozell, and Clyde Wilcox. 2003. *The Christian Right in American Politics: Marching to the Millennium.* Georgetown: Georgetown University Press.

Hassan, Hassan. 2016. *The sectarianism of the Islamic state: Ideological roots and political context.* Washington, DC: Carnegie Endowment for International Peace. https://carnegieendowment.org/research/2016/12/the-sectarianism-of-the-islamic-state-ideological-roots-and-political-context?lang=en

Haynes, Jeffrey. 2019. *From Huntington to Trump: Thirty Years of the Clash of Civilizations.* Lanham: Lexington Books.

Haynes, Jeffrey. 2023. 'Christian Nationalism and Politics in Ghana', *Religions,* 14, 9:1202. https://doi.org/10.3390/rel14091202

Haynes, Jeffrey, Peter Hough, and Bruce Pilbeam. 2023. *World Politics: International Relations and Globalisation in the 21st Century,* 3rd ed. London: Sage.

Hobsbawm, Eric. 1990. *On Nationalism.* New York: Little Brown.

Kuenkler, Mirjam, John Madeley, and Shylashri Shankar (eds.). 2019. *A Secular Age beyond the West: Religion, Law, and the State in Asia, the Middle East, and North Africa.* Cambridge: Cambridge University Press.

Little, David. 1994. 'Religious nationalism and human rights', in G. F. Powers, D. Christiansen and R. Hennemeyer (eds.), *Peacemaking: Moral and Policy Challenges for a New World.* Washington: US Catholic Conference, 84–95.

Mahdi, N. 2006. 'Reconciling faith and loyalty to country. Address to the 30th Annual Convention of the Ahmadiyya Muslim Community of Canada, July 9, 2006'. Accessed 17 March 2009. www.ahmadiyya.ca/speeches/Reconciling_Faith_and_Loyalty_to_Country.pdf

Malji, Andrea. 2021. 'How Buddhist nationalism is shaping Sri Lanka's domestic and foreign policy'. *9Dashline.* www.9dashline.com/article/how-buddhist-nationalism-is-shaping-sri-lanka-domestic-and-foreign-policy

Marchetti, Raffaele. 2016. *Global Strategic Engagement.* Lanham: Lexington Books.

Ommerborn, W. (2003) 'The importance of universal principles in Confucianism and the problems connected to Jiang Qing's concept of political Confucianism and his theory of particular principles'. www.ekohaus.de/menzius/universal.htm#_ftnref3]%20

Pew Research Center. 2019. 'In U.S., decline of Christianity continues at rapidpace', 17 October. www.pewresearch.org/religion/2019/10/17/in-u-s-decline-of-christianity-continues-at-rapid-pace/

Smith, Anthony D. 2003. *Chosen Peoples. Sacred Sources of National Identity*. Oxford: Oxford University Press.

Wald, Kenneth. 1991. 'Social change and political response the silent religious cleavage in North America', in George Moyser (ed.), *Religion and Politics in the Modern World*. London: Routledge, 239–84.

Weber, Max. 1969. 'Major features of world religions' in Roland Robertson (ed.), *Sociology of Religion*. Baltimore: Penguin, 19–41.

Whitehead, Andrew, and Samuel Perry. 2020. *Taking America Back for God: Christian Nationalism in the United States*. Oxford: Oxford University Press.

CHALLENGES AND OPPORTUNITIES

My first book on politics and religion, *Religion in Third World Politics*,[1] was published in 1993 (Haynes 1993). It was among the first of an array of books covering what then seemed to many a surprising new phenomenon: the 'return' of political religion to the public realm. Over the next three decades, there was increased scholarly and policy makers' attention paid to the various ways that politics impacts on religion, and *vice versa*, both in and between states around the world. This attention was stimulated and furthered by a series of events, following Iran's Islamic Revolution of 1979, a subsequent generalised rise of political Islam in the Middle East and North Africa (MENA), and the implosion of communism in the Soviet Empire in the late 1980s/early 1990s. These events in particular ensured that the topic of politics and religion remained central to the concerns of at least some political scientists, including the present author.

Iran's 1979 revolution was especially important in reminding political scientists of the power of religion to influence political outcomes in various parts of the world. The Iranian revolution indicated that a religious movement could overthrow a regime once seen as the regional exemplar of secularisation and modernisation and go on to establish and consolidate in power a modern religious and revolutionary party, the Islamic Republic Party (IRP). In the United States at roughly the same time, the rise of the Christian Right indicated that religious movements can evolve in tandem with political parties, significantly changing political

DOI: 10.4324/9781003508823-8

outcomes (Wilcox and Robinson 2007). In addition, the role of the Pope and the Catholic Church in supporting Solidarity in Poland during the late 1980s/early 1990s ably demonstrated the power of religious groups to encourage social movements and parties to challenge non-democratic regimes and help introduce democratic politics to previously non-democratic countries. Moreover, contrary to what many assume, the church's more complex role with post-independence political parties in Poland shows that democracy does not simplify the relationships between religious institutions and political parties (Byrnes 2001). Instead, it makes politics more complex as religion – in this case, Catholicism – influences political issues and debates in a number of ways.

This book has sought to examine key issues in the relationship between politics and religion in the 'real world' today. In 2025, religion's social and political significance and influence is universal. While its impact varies from country to country, religion is now much more consistently sociopolitically significant today compared to 50 or 60 years ago. How and why is religion now politically 'significant'? This has come about mainly because religion encourages, or helps resolve, often interlinked political, social, economic and developmental disagreements and conflicts. Religion has important functions, serving to engender and/or significantly influence individual and group values that, in turn, impact upon common existential issues. Such issues may lead to irresolvable conflict within countries; sometimes they spill over to become serious regional or international concerns. In both cases, they impact the state and people's security. To comprehend political issues involving religion both within countries and internationally, the book keeps in view two overlapping, but conceptually distinct, issues: governance and security.

Focusing on today and in some cases seeking to extrapolate to the next few decades, the book's chapters have identified and examined emerging trends of strategic importance to our understanding of politics and religion. Centrally informed by the centrality of religion's influence – affecting individual identity, society and governance – we start from the observation that for billions of people around the world their religion is the most important signifier of their identity. But religion does not act in isolation and in recent years two key developments have led to increased religious responses in many parts of the world. On the one hand, the expansion – and in some cases, reversal – of representative government to all global regions via democratisation, with the important exception of the MENA, has provided new political and social space for religion to be assertive. On the other hand, because religion is so fundamental to many people's identity, opening political and social space has often encouraged new or pre-existing tensions to surface or resurface, leading in some cases to inter-group conflicts, expressed both domestically and in relation to international politics.

Overall, the chapters of the book underline the following:

- Politically assertive religion impacts upon governance and security outcomes within many countries, as well as internationally.
- Globalisation and associated technology, including satellite television channels and social media, play an important role in spreading sectarian and inter-faith mistrust.
- Factionalism within religious traditions can exacerbate societal tensions, both within countries and internationally.
- High levels of economic and developmental inequality – linked to religion, ethnicity and/or class – endure as sources of regional and international tension, including in Sub-Saharan Africa, the MENA, Central Asia, South and East Asia, Western Europe and North and South America.
- Sectarian and other inter-religious tensions reflect longstanding socio-economic disparities which escalate when governments fail adequately to deal with them.
- Sectarian conflicts deepen pre-existing religious divides which in some cases escalate into serious national, regional or international conflicts, deleteriously affecting governance and political and social stability.

POLITICS, RELIGION AND SECURITY

The first decades of the twenty-first century have seen numerous examples of politicised forms of religion, both within countries and internationally. This development affects all the 'world religions' (Buddhism, Christianity, Confucianism, Hinduism, Islam and Judaism). With hindsight, we can see that the 'resurgence' of politicised forms of religion started several decades ago, with the Iranian revolution of 1979. This epochal event had national, regional and international impacts, comprising a form of revolution which changed our understanding of the political roles of religion. Within Iran, it led to a unique form of government, which endures to this day, ending an experiment in Western-style modernisation, which, like in Turkey, following the collapse of the Ottoman Empire soon after World War I, was posited on the apparent strength and desirability of a strongly secular, pro-Western, development model. Regionally, Iran's revolution exacerbated Sunni/Shia tensions and conflicts. Internationally, Iran's revolution highlighted religion's transnational political significance, whereby Iran's revolutionary government, rather like Russia's revolutionary government after the overthrow of the Tsar in 1917, sought to export revolution to further the country's national interests. Iran's revolution led to continuing rivalry with a regional 'Sunni' power, Saudi Arabia, affecting relations with, *inter alia*, Bahrain, Iraq, Syria and Yemen. Consequent to Iran's revolution, the US political scientist, Samuel Huntington (2002; also see Haynes 2019), claimed to see a 'clash of civilisations', centrally involving Christianity and Islam, because of supposedly clashing values and norms. Many critiqued Huntington's argument, yet it is impossible to deny that his 'clash of civilisations' thesis and associated rhetoric has helped further perceptions of a globalised division between 'the West' and 'Islam', with significant impacts on security and governance issues both within countries and internationally (Haynes 2019).

Recent decades have been characterised by growing political assertiveness of several world religions, notably Christianity and Islam. Political assertiveness is manifested both within countries, as well as internationally and transnationally. Central to this development is the phenomenon of globalisation and associated developments in communications technology. The latter permits religious entities' messages to unite or divide real or imagined communities, even when physically separated by international borders and thousands of kilometres. In particular, it enables diaspora populations to feel a closeness otherwise denied them and appeals to a far wider audience than previously possible. Globalisation technology based on the internet is also likely to contribute to diaspora communities being increasingly affected by intra-faith discord in countries of origin, such as Pakistan and India. In addition, some governments may have to address new challenges from religious groups at home. For example, it is posited that over the next two decades, China will be home to some of the world's largest Muslim and Christian populations. The impact on China's internal politics and global attitude and focus are likely to be influenced significantly by the manner in which these two faith groups pursue their goals and seek enhanced religious freedoms. A wider point is that as religion is so fundamental to many people's identity, where tensions between different groups already exist, they may be exacerbated by real or imagined religious differences.

Post-Cold War globalisation has led to dramatic, continuing increases in interactions between people and communities, no longer dependent on geographical closeness easily to enable such connections. Globalisation encourages religions to adopt new, revised or reformed social, moral and/or political agendas. It stimulates many religious individuals, organisations and movements to look not only at local and national issues and contexts but also to focus on regional and international environments, which, in many countries of the developing world, often link into or exacerbate pre-existing negative perceptions of foreign – including, US and Western – cultural, political and economic hegemonies. Moreover, encounters between different religious traditions, both within faiths and between them, are increasingly common and not always harmonious. Sometimes the result can be extreme hostility, captured in the term 'culture wars'.

Culture wars in countries as diverse as Israel and the United States occur in relation to pronounced, potentially irreconcilable, differences between secular and religious groups regarding the appropriate positions of religious and secular norms, values and behaviour. Culture wars also occur when differing religious worldviews encourage different allegiances and standards in relation to various areas, including the family, law, education and politics. As a result, conflicts involving, *inter alia*, gender, ethnicity, class and nations are often framed religiously. Such conflicts may 'take on "larger-than-life" proportions, depicted as the struggle of good against evil' (Kurtz 1995), impacting security, sometimes dramatically, both within counties and internationally. This is also the case with some religious minorities who may regard their own existential position – for example, Muslim minority communities in the United Kingdom, France, the Philippines and India, and Christian minorities in many countries in the MENA – to be unacceptably weakened because of actual or perceived pressure from majority religious communities, such as Buddhists in Thailand, Christians in the United Kingdom, France, and the Philippines, and Hindus in India, which encourage religious minorities to conform to the hegemonic norms and values of the religious and cultural majority.

This issue has recently affected a region long thought to be immune to the public impact of religion and culture: Western Europe. There, governments long ago went down the path of secularisation, with linked 'downgrading' of religion from public realm to privatised belief. Today, however, many urban areas across Western Europe contain areas of pronounced social deprivation, often the home to many migrants. Recent extensive migration to Western Europe from the MENA and elsewhere in the global south, coupled with enhanced global mobility, resulted in multicultural societies, albeit often within a wider trend towards secularism. Yet, local communities with strong religious beliefs continue to exist and, due to natural expansion, are growing in size. Recent political developments, such as the rise of the Reform Party in the United Kingdom and Alternative for Germany in Germany, highlight that many, perhaps most, Western Europeans at best *tolerate* – not actively *embrace* and *welcome* – migrants from the global south. Suspicion and hostility are particularly apparent in times of economic stress – for example, since 2008 and the latest international economic collapse – when many Western Europeans appear to revert to older societal affiliations, including reference to cultural models of Christianity, said to exemplify and underline two key components underpinning modern (Western) European culture: liberal and individualistic values. For some, especially on the political right, this sets apart Western European culture from what is regarded as less liberal, more conservative values and norms of Europe's Muslim immigrants from the global south.

The issue is a perceived security threat within Western Europe and internationally. Future projections are that the population growth of non-Muslims in Europe will be slow, while the Muslim population of Europe is expected to continue to grow, exceeding 58 million by 2030 (i.e. approximately 8% of the total population), but with numbers of people claiming to adhere to Christian traditions (primarily Protestant, Catholic or Orthodox) not expanding. Reflecting the impact of globalisation and internet-based communications technologies, diaspora Muslim communities in Western Europe are likely to be increasingly affected by intra-faith and intra-Islamic discord emanating from the MENA. Tensions between Sunni and Shias are likely to spread. For example, in 2012, hard-line locally based Sunnis firebombed Belgium's largest Shiite mosque.

Several countries in the MENA are regional focal points of religious actors' increased political involvement. On the one hand, religious minorities across the region, including in the region's largest country by population, Egypt, are squeezed and their security compromised. While 'Islamic fundamentalism' or 'Islamism' attracts much attention, there is also serious sectarian division and conflict across much of MENA, including in Syria, Iraq and Yemen, as well as in Pakistan and Afghanistan. The situation was exacerbated by the 2010s Arab Uprisings and their aftermath, leading to widespread regional state weakness or failure which, combined with the impact of politically assertive religious actors, led to increasing pressure on religious minorities to convert to the dominant religious tradition or, failing that, to flee for their lives.

Extremist actors such as Islamic State and al Qaeda thrive on, and seek to perpetuate and deepen, sectarian divisions. The resumption of power in Afghanistan of the Taliban in 2021, the removal of American influence from the country, and the assassination of the al Qaeda leader, Ayman al-Zawahiri, in a drone strike in Kabul in mid-2022, highlight that the forces that gave rise to conflict with the West as highlighted by 9/11, are still around, and capable of producing significant impacts on both domestic and international political outcomes.

Given the widespread diminution of state capacity in the MENA following the Arab Uprisings of the early 2010s and the linked expansion of aggressive Sunni entities, such as Islamic State, then it is likely that the short and medium term will see significant sectarian conflicts in regional countries, leading to significant friction and, in some cases, conflicts between warring sectarian groups. There is also a notable regional and international dimension to these issues. There are significant tensions between Shia-majority Iran and the (Sunni-dominated) Gulf Cooperation Council. However, not all regional Shia movements are pro-Iranian and not every Salafist or Wahhabist Sunni movement kowtows to Saudi Arabia. Indeed, there are significant Shiite minorities in GCC countries, as well as a growing (Sunni) Salafi movement in Iran. Sectarian tensions reflect socio-economic disparities and seem destined to escalate if governments continue to address existential economic and development. For example, in both Bahrain and Saudi Arabia, where there is pronounced economic inequality between Sunni and Shia Muslims, tensions are likely to rise with unclear consequences. In addition, globalisation, characterised by influential satellite television channels and social media, plays a pivotal role in spreading anti-government rhetoric and sectarian mistrust. Finally, the next few decades are also likely to see growing tensions *within* Sunni and Shiite communities. Sunni Islam is become increasingly factionalised. As Salafist groups grow in prominence, a backlash may emerge from moderate Sunnis. Correspondingly, Shiite Islam contains a number of internal divisions.

The countries in the MENA that have suffered most from decades of systematic political, sectarian and racial repression and mass killings – such as Iraq and Syria – made possible the foundation, emergence and development of Islamic State. What makes these countries' situation even more dire is the failure of the 'international community' consistently to condemn this oppression, in effect turning a blind eye to the roots of Islamic State-style radicalisation, and failing, due to political considerations at home, to help meaningfully to deal with the real and present existential threat that Islamic State still poses, despite its recent reversals. Yet, it is no longer about a choice between countering terrorism and respecting human rights. It is impossible to win the fight against terror in the region without addressing the oppression and lack of opportunity that encourages it. Defending human rights and confronting religious extremism, working to end the discrimination against Syrian and Iraqi Sunni populations, as well as against the Bedouins of Sinai, would be the necessary first steps in a long journey to deal with human rights violations in MENA and, as a result, begin to undermine the attraction of Islamic State and similar ideological entities for tens of thousands of alienated young people.

Whereas in Western Europe Muslim minority populations question their social and cultural position and in MENA state breakdown encourages sectarian strife and the persecution of religious minorities, in 'secular' Central Asia Islamist movements represent a challenge to the status quo. This is not because they are especially powerful: today they stand almost no chance of overpowering state institutions or gathering substantial support in urban areas. Yet, regional governments have sought to combat what they see as extremism in a heavy-handed manner, which has exacerbated the problem that Islamist movements see themselves fighting against: poor, corrupt and repressive ruling regimes. Many Central Asian governments are Western-friendly and, while Islamism is likely to remain a long-term (if low-level) threat to stability, it does highlight to many ordinary Central Asians that the West is a friend to their often highly disliked governments. Continued socio-economic adversity and growing animosity towards an overbearing, monopolistic state is likely to increase the number of instances of instability across Central Asia. Social discontent may result in support for underground religious movements rather than opposition parties, while strengthening anti-Western feeling in many Central Asian countries.

POLITICS, RELIGION, GOVERNANCE AND GLOBAL ORDER

In 2025, many people see the world in the midst of serious disorder, consequent to the Covid-19 pandemic, Russia's continuing war in Ukraine, and associated economic travails, including high price inflation and natural resource shortages. Then there is the grotesque spectacle of the climate emergency and associated environmental catastrophes being treated as a 'hoax' by right-wingers around the world.

Recent analyses of religion and politics highlight the relevance of such issues, as well as the economic range and social and cultural significance of transnational business corporations (TNCs) (Haynes, Hough and Pilbeam 2023). There is a widespread perception that TNCs today have more power than many governments and are largely beyond democratic control. Whether TNCs improve or exacerbate mass impoverishment of already poor people in countries around the world is a contested issue. Numerous religious organisations, including, for example, the 350-member World Council of Churches, now focus on global and domestic economic imbalances and suggest ways to ameliorate them using the power of religious organisation and community. Religion concern is manifested in various ways, including new religious fundamentalisms; support for anti-globalisation activities, such as recent anti-globalisation and anti-World Trade Organisation protests; and North/South economic justice efforts, including the Millennium Development Goals (2000–15) and the Sustainable Development Goals (2015–30). In short, recent religious responses to what are perceived as an unacceptable – yet potentially amendable – result of economic globalisation highlight – yet again – the potential power of religion to be a globally significant public actor with (potential or actual) ability to impact significantly on global issues.

This observation draws on a recognition that around the world many religious organisations and (secular) development agencies share similar concerns: (1) how to improve the lot of materially poor people, (2) the societal position of those suffering from social exclusion and (3) widely unfulfilled human potential in the context of glaring developmental polarisation within and between countries, a position which international financial institutions, such as the World Bank, accept is untenable. Developmental concerns focus upon, but are not confined to, issues linked to poverty, HIV/AIDS, conflict, gender concerns, international trade and global politics. These issues explicitly link all the world's countries and peoples – rich and poor – into a global community. How to resolve them poses a challenge to governance and global order. In this context, religious authorities and actors increasingly raise their voices, although it is unclear whether decision-makers, both within countries and internationally, take them seriously enough to take their views into account.

Challenges to the status quo manifest themselves in the actions of some extremist religious organisations whose impact upon Western interests is explicitly hostile and very difficult to counter. They are likely to get worse over the coming decades – *unless* coordinated, concerted efforts are made to blunt their impact by ameliorating the conditions which give rise to them. For example, al Qaeda has a stronghold in Yemen, while Islamic State is still influential in various countries, including Syria and Iraq, and controls the 'State of Sinai', an area of Egypt outside the jurisdiction of central government. For a while, IS controlled the city of Derna in Libya, but was ousted. In 2025, IS continues a 'roving insurgency' without a territorial base but with a transcontinental alliance with Boko Haram in Nigeria.

In Nigeria, Boko Haram is a long-running regional threat to security. Premised upon the claim that 'Western education is forbidden', in order to deny girls the right to an education, Boko Haram is an apparently indiscriminate killer organisation, making no distinction between followers of different religions. Yet, Boko Haram cannot be understood in isolation. To a significant extent, the organisation is an outcome of decades of the absence of good governance leading to severe social injustices, rampant Islamist and Christian extremism, and sweeping human rights violations.

The example of Boko Haram highlights how religion, along with culture, ethnicity and identity, are important components in understanding governance and global order issues, while contextualising post-9/11 Western counter-insurgency efforts. Following 9/11, first al Qaeda and its affiliates and then Islamic State and its allies sequentially posed serious threats to governance in many countries and by extension global order and Western security. While it is well known that al Qaeda perpetrated multiple attacks against US and Western targets in the 1990s and early 2000s, these outrages raised questions about the ideological assumptions and goals of al Qaeda. While Bin Laden was personally committed to the fight against the 'far enemy' – the USA – Islamic State seeks to target the 'near enemy': ideologically and 'un-Islamic' governments and populations in the MENA. However, given that many of the dead in the attacks are not Western Christians or Jews but local Muslims, it raises the question of what exactly the perpetrators are seeking to achieve. What today are the ideological assumptions and goals of what is left of al Qaeda, Islamic State and their regional affiliates, such as Boko Haram? Al Qaeda first emerged in the late 1980s to challenge the incumbency and authority of rulers in various Middle Eastern countries, including Saudi Arabia, with the objective of replacing them with plausibly 'Islamic' leaders. Over time, however, a lack of success in achieving these objectives led al Qaeda strategists to shift attention to regional and global goals, including taking the fight, on 9/11, to the 'far enemy' (Gerges 2005). The result is a continuing 'anti-Western' conflict, seeking to utilise various 'weapons of terror', a campaign more recently adopted by the down-but-not-out Islamic State. Both al Qaeda and Islamic State share concerns about spreading the 'right' religion by jihad, and the global balance of power currently dominated by the USA and the West. Over time, wars in Iraq and Afghanistan, as well as more recent – and in some cases continuing – conflicts in Mali, Nigeria and Syria, indicate that religion, culture and identity are continuing concerns of many conflicts. In each case, there are explicit links to long-term and systemic governance shortfalls, which have to be ameliorated before the threat from extremist Islam can be nullified and the threat to the West's security significantly reduced.

CONCLUSION

How best to understand interactions of politics and religion in the aftermath of what some see as a worldwide religious revival? How best to conclude our brief survey of the basics of politics and religion in 2025? It is clear that we live in a hierarchical and multipolar, but also interdependent and multilateral, global system. Its development is contextualised by events of the last three decades or so, that is, since the game-changing end of the Cold War. For most political scientists, however, religion is rarely a 'game changer'. Having said that, its various manifestations – expressed in the actions and reactions of both states and transnational non-state actors and captured in specific events, such as the Iranian revolution, 9/11 and their aftermaths – can, at times and in relation to certain issues, be highly significant, significantly affecting national, regional and/or international outcomes. It does not follow, however, that religion's 'return' to political significance means that we must fundamentally adjust our understanding of how politics works or political science is theorised. The study of politics' enduring fascination with states has not been side-lined by the advent – or return – of religion to the analytical frame. States are still highly important, and most are always or very often secular in both national and international policies. When it comes to religion's impact on politics today, evidence suggests that existing – mainly secular – political science theories have not been superseded, despite the fact that, collectively, they see little or no consistent significance for religion. Today, in the aftermath of a widespread – some would say global – religious revival, the myriad relationships between religion and politics remain an intriguing so far unresolved opaque component of how we understand our world.

NOTE

1 The 'First World' was the West, the 'Second World' was the Soviet Union and associated communist allies, and the 'Third World' was the remaining countries, mainly located in the global south.

REFERENCES

Byrnes, Timothy. 2001. *Transnational Catholicism in Postcommunist Europe.* Lanham: Rowman & Littlefield.

Gerges, Fawaz A. 2005. *The Far Enemy: Why Jihad Went Global.* New York: Cambridge University Press.

Haynes, Jeffrey. 1993. *Religion in Third World Politics.* Milton Keynes: Open University Press.

Haynes, Jeffrey. 2019. *From Huntington to Trump: Thirty Years of the Clash of Civilizations*. New York: Lexington Books.

Haynes, Jeffrey, Peter Hough and Bruce Pilbeam. 2023. *World Politics: International Relations and Globalisation in the 21st Century*, 3rd ed. London: Sage.

Huntington, Samuel. 2002. *The Clash of Civilizations and the Remaking of World Order,* New ed. New York: Free Press.

Kurtz, Lester. 1995. *Gods in the Global Village: The World's Religions in Sociological Perspective*. New York: Sage.

Wilcox, Clyde, and Carin Robinson. 2007. 'The faith of George W. Bush: The personal, practical, and political', in Mark J. Rozell and Gleaves Whitney (eds.) *Religion and the American Presidency*. New York: Palgrave/MacMillan, 215–38.

INDEX

Note: Endnotes are indicated by the page number followed by "n" and the note number e.g., 111n5 refers to note 5 on page 111.

9/11 (al Qaeda attack on the USA on 11 September 2001) 49–50, 57, 61, 75, 81–82, 84–85, 139, 162–163, 166–167, 168; *see also* al Qaeda

Afghanistan: Soviet invasion of 50; subordination of Muslim females 99; Taliban in 140, 162; theocracy in 5, 28, 46 (box), 140; Western involvement in 57
African countries: religious nonbelievers in 129–130; weak civil societies 37
al Qaeda 9, 20, 49, 50, 62, 81, 84–85, 150, 162, 166–167; *see also* 9/11 (al Qaeda attack on the USA on 11 September 2001)
al-Zawahiri, Ayman 162
Albania 31–32

Algeria 28; state discrimination against Christian minorities 119; transformative minority politics 120(box); war of independence 105
Alternative for Germany 161
Amazigh 120 (box)
American Revolution 48, 56–57
Anthony, D. 79 (box)
anti-semitism in MENA countries 121–122
Arab Uprisings (2011) 69, 70, 121, 162, 163
Argentina, relatively strong civil societies 38
Aslan, Reza 93–94
Aslanidis, Paris 94
atheism/Atheists 127–128, 129; China teaching Tibetan Buddhists 32

Australia: as 'post-secular' 59 (box); right-wing populist nationalists 76, 136, 138; secularisation 5
Ayatollah Khomeini 29 (box)

Bala, Mubarak 127–128
Bangladesh, Hindu population 15
Bardakcioglu, Ali 103
Bellah, Robert 79–80, 79 (box)
Bharatiya Janata Party (BJP) 27, 31, 76–77, 143 (box)
Bhutan: Buddhist population 12; Hindu population 15
bin Laden, Osama 9, 50, 167
Black Lives Matter (BLM) 81
Boko Haram 166–167
Bolsanaro, Jair 72 (box)
Boswell, Christina 6
Brazil 72–73 (box); 'Evangelical Caucus' 72 (box); evangelical Protestantism 72 (box); UN human rights resolution 125
Broken Covenant, The (Bellah) 80
Brubaker, Rogers 139
Buddhism: political importance 141–142; Tibetan Buddhists 32; as world religion 12–13
Burke, Jason 82
Burma (Myanmar) 84, 141–142
Bush, George W. 47 (box), 85, 115
Buzan, Barry 138

Cambodia, Buddhist population 12
Canada: as 'post-secular' 59 (box); right-wing nationalists 138; secularisation 5
Capital Women's Platform *(Baskent Kadin Platform)*, Turkey 103–104
Capitol building attack 6 January 2021 84
Casanova, José 23, 31, 71
Catholicism in Brazil 72 (box)

Central and Eastern Europe, significant role of civil society 37
Central Asia: revival of Islam in 32; weak civil societies 37; Western-friendly governments 164
Charles III, king 24
Chile, relatively strong civil societies 38
China: challenges from religious groups 160; communism in 32; Confucianism in 14, 32, 144–145; growth of Christianity 47 (box)
Christendom, transnational religious society 52
Christian conservatives 77, 86n2; groups at UN 123–124 (box)
Christian nationalism 145, 147, 148 (box)
Christian Right 46–47 (box), 77, 80–81, 86n2, 123 (box), 142, 147, 156
Christianity, as world religion 11, 13
Church of England 24; non-state religious actor 49
civil religion: and culture wars in USA 78–79 (box); state and in USA 23–24 (box)
civil society 25, 35–39; contrast to political society 36; definition 36–37; democratic transitions 36; religion in 38; three broad categories 37–38
'clash of civilisations' 57, 61, 75, 85, 159
Clinton, Bill 114–115
Cold War 49, 50, 57, 62, 67, 68 (box), 82, 114, 130, 138, 142, 144, 160, 168

colonialism 47–48, 53; Christianity and 52 (box); secular ideologies and European 68 (box)
communications revolution 53–54 (box)
communism 25; collapse in Central and Eastern Europe 37
communist-secular states 31–32
Confucianism: nationalism and 144–145; as world religion 14; worldwide population 14
Connell, Raewyn 93
contentious politics: culture wars 77–81; definition 66 (box); democratisation and democracy 71–74; disruptive techniques 66 (box); and religion 67–70; religious terrorism 81–85; right-wing populism 74–77
Costa Rica, party system 34
covenant (Judaism) 17
Cuba 32
culture wars 77–81, 160–161
Czech Republic, relatively strong civil societies 38

Daesh 81, 84, 85, 86n4 *see also* Islamic State
dawla 27, 86n4
decolonisation 46 (box), 67, 68 (box), 142
democratic transitions 33–34, 36
democratisation 32–35, 71–74; third wave of 33, 36, 39, 53
discrimination: Jews 121–122; non-religious in sub-Saharan Africa 125–130; women and sexual minoroties 122–125
disruptive techniques 66 (box)
Diyanet (Turkey) 103
Duda, Andrzej 124

Egypt 96–97; Freedom and Justice Party 69; increased sectarian tensions 121; state discrimination against Christian minorities 119
elections 33, 34, 36, 71
End of History and the Last Man, The (Fukuyama) 68–69
England, established church in 24, 30–31
Ennahda (Tunisia) 69
Erdoğan, President Recep Tayyip 31
Europe, as 'post-secular' 59 (box)
European expansionism 52 (box)
European Network against Racism (ENAR) 106–107
Evangelical Caucus, Brazil 72 (box)
Evangelical Protestantism 38; Brazil 72 (box)

Feminism 90–108; France 104–107; Islamic 98–102; and religion 90 (box); Turkey 102–104
Fiji, Hindu population 15
Focus on the Family group 124
Fox, Jonathan 58, 61, 114, 116, 122
France: colonialism and 52 (box); Islamic feminism 104–107; laïcité (secularism), 106; Muslim population in 104–105; state and church in 25–26 (box); strong civil society 38
Freedom and Justice Party (Egypt) 69
freedom of religion or belief (FoRB) 112–116, 119, 122, 130
French Revolution 48, 56–57; terrorism 83–84
Fukuyama, Francis 68–69

Gay & Lesbian Alliance against Defamation 123 (box)
Gellner, Ernest 139
gender 90–108; challenges facing Arab/Muslim women 100 (box); ideology and 94–98; and politics 90–92; power and 93–94
'generally religious' states 30
Germany: as 'post-secular' 59 (box); Reformation and 56; strong civil society 38
Ghana: Christian Nationalism in 148 (box); multi-religious state 31; secular constitution 125–126 (box)
global order *see* governance and global order
Global War on Terror 85
globalisation 51–55, 160; definition 54; 'global culture' 53; technological revolution key component 51, 159–160
governance and global order 164–167
Greece, 'third wave of democratisation' 33
Gregg, Heather S. 83
Gulf Cooperation Council 163
Guyana, Hindu population 15

Habermas, Jürgen 59 (box)
hadiths 102–103, 149
Hamas 121
headscarves 99, 104, 105
Hegel, Georg Wilhelm Friedrich 36
hijab 105
Hindu nationalism 76–77, 83
Hindu Rashtra 77
Hinduism: lack of church 27; as world religion 14–15; worldwide population 14

Hindutva 76–77
Hobsbawm, Eric 139
Holy See 96, 97
Hong Kong, Confucianism in 14
human rights: Eleanor Roosevelt and 112–113 (box); freedom of religion or belief 112–116; UN conferences on 95–96
Huntington, Samuel 8, 57, 61, 76, 85, 138, 159
Hurrell, Andrew 82

ideology 94–98; 'thick' and 'thin' ideologies 94
immigration: anti-immigration stance of USA 136–137; France 104–105; Western Europe 161
India: 2019 abrogation of Article 370 77; Hindu population 14–15; multi-religious state 31; party system 34; right-wing populism 75; strong civil society 38 *see also* Bharatiya Janata Party (BJP)
Indian National Congress 27
Indonesia: 'generally religious' state 30; Hindu population 15
International Convention on Elimination of All Forms of Racial Discrimination 114
International Covenant on Civil and Political Rights (ICCPR) 113–114
International Monetary Fund 41
international politics: after World War II 46–47 (box); globalisation 51–55; post-secular 58–61; and religion 55–58
International Religious Freedom Act (IRFA) 115, 131n1
Iran: state discrimination against Christian minorities 119;

theocracy in 28, 29–30 (box), 46 (box); unique form of government 159; war with Iraq 29 (box)
Iranian revolution (1979) 4–5, 17–18, 29–30 (box), 49, 61, 70, 81, 156, 159, 168
Iraq: Islamic feminism 99; state discrimination against Christian minorities 119; Western involvement in 57
Islam: expanded from Arabian heartland 51–52; Jerusalem as holy city of 48 (box); Mohammed 15–16, 102, 103; political Islam (Islamism) 69; state and 27–28; theocracies 28; as world religion 15–16; worldwide population 15
Islamic feminism 98–102; France 104–107; Turkey 102–104
Islamic Republic Party (Iran) 29–30 (box), 70, 156
Islamic State 29 (box), 49, 62, 84, 85, 150–151, 162, 163–164, 166–167 see also Daesh
Islamic terrorism 82, 83, 84
Israel 16; religion and democracy 48 (box)

Jammu and Kashmir 77
Japan: Buddhist population 12; Confucianism in 14
Jerusalem 48 (box)
Jiang Qing 145
Jordan, honour killings 99
Judaism: anti-semitism in MENA countries 121–122; several meanings 17; as world religion 16–17; worldwide population 16
Justice and Development Party (*Adalet ve Kalkınma Partisi;* AKP), Turkey 31, 76

Kano state (Nigeria) 127–128
Kay, Zara 128
Kenya, denial of rights of non-believers 129
Khatami, Mohammad 30 (box)
Korea, Confucianism in 14

laïcité (secularism), France 106
Laos, Buddhist population 12
Latin America: church-state relations 26; exclusion of study of religion in gender studies 97–98 (box); Protestant evangelical surge 47 (box); Roman Catholic Church 26, 47 (box)
League of Nations 117
LGBTQ people, discrimination against 122–125
Libya, Western involvement in 57
Lord's Resistance Army (Uganda) 83

Malaysia, Hindu population 15
Marchetti, Raffaele 137 (box), 138
Martin, Gus 82–83
Mauritius, Hindu population 15
Mbiti, John 125
McAdam, Doug 66 (box)
Mecca 16, 99, 151; Islamic feminism 99
Middle East and North Africa (MENA) 69; discrimination against religious minorities 118–122; focal points of religious actors 162; Islamic renaissance 47 (box); Islamic State in 163–164; sectarian division and conflict 162
Middle Eastern countries, weak civil societies 37
Millennium Development Goals 165

INDEX 175

minorities, religious *see* religious minorities
Mintrom, Michael 91
Modi, Narendra 27, 31, 77
Mohammed 15–16, 102, 103
Moral Majority 80, 147
Morlino, Leonardo 34
Morocco 69
mullahs 27, 30 (box)
Mumai, Harrison 129
Mundy, Jacob 120 (box)
Muslim Brotherhood 150–151
Myanmar, Buddhist population 12

Nasser, Gamal Abdel 151
National Organisation for Intelligence and Security (*Sazeman-i Ettelaat va Amniyat-i Keshvar*, known as SAVAK) 29 (box)
nationalism: Christianity and 145–148; and Confucianism 144–145; Islam and 148–151; and religion 139–145; secular 135–139
Nepal 68; Hindu population 15
Netherlands, as 'post-secular' 59 (box)
New Christian Right (NCR) 81
New Zealand, 'post-secular' 59 (box)
Nigeria, Boko Haram 166–167
non-believers 125–130; denial of rights in Nigeria 127–128; stigmatisation in Africa 126–127
North Korea 32

Obama, Barack 115
Orbán, Viktor 137
Organisation of the Islamic Conference, non-state religious actor 49
Öztürk, Ahmed Erdi 61

Pakistan, Hindu population 15
Pancasila 30, 43n1
Party of Justice and Development (Morocco) 69
Peace of Westphalia 47, 52(box), 56, 116
Pearse, Rebecca 93
Peru 68
Philpott, Daniel 56
Poland: 'generally religious' state 30; LGBTQ rights 124; Roman Catholic Church support for Solidarity 70, 157
political Islam (Islamism) 69
political parties 33–34
political society 32–35
politics, definitions of 6–8
Pompeo, Mike 115, 123 (box)
populism, left/right wing 74 (box)
Portugal: colonialism and 52 (box); 'third wave of democratisation' 33
post-secular international politics 58–61
Putnam, Robert 39, 39–40 (box)

Qur'an 29 (box), 99, 101–102, 101 (box), 104, 149
Qutb, Sayyid 150–151

Reform Party (UK) 161
Reformation 26–27
relatively strong civil societies 38
religion, definitions of 8–10
Religion in Third World Politics (Haynes) 156
religious actor: in civil society 38; definition 63n1; international politics 49, 55
religious minorities, discrimination against in MENA countries 118–122

religious nationalism 140–142, 148 (box)
religious symbols in schools 106
religious terrorism 81–85
resacralisation 60, 63n2
Reveyrand-Coulon, Odie 99
right-wing nationalists 75, 137 (box), 138, 139
right-wing populism 74–77; anti-elitist sentiments 75–76; characteristics of parties 75–76; "clash of civilizations" 75; discrimination against religious minorities 119; superior civilisations 76
Risse-Kappen, Thomas 37
Robbins, T. 79 (box)
Roman Catholic Church 106; France 25–26 (box); Latin America 26; non-state religious actor 49; Spain and Poland 30; supporting Solidarity in Poland 70
Roosevelt, Eleanor 112–113 (box)
Rousseau, Jean-Jacques 78–79 (box)
Russia, war in Ukraine 164–165

Salih, Mohamed 128
Sandal, Nukhet 58, 61, 76
Sanskrit 15
Sartori, Giovanni 33–34
satellite television channels 158, 163
Saudi Arabia 96, 163; state discrimination against Christian minorities 119; theocracy in 28, 46 (box)
schools 129
Scott, James C. 66 (box)
secular ideologies and European colonisation 68 (box)

secular nationalism 135–139
secular power: Israel as secular state 48 (box); perceived superiority of 48; principles applied in international politics 49
secular white conservatives 77–78
secularisation 3–5, 26, 31, 35, 59–60, 59 (box), 70 *see also* post-secular international politics; 'unsecularization of the world'
security 158–164
Seiple, Chris 56
sexual and reproductive health rights (SRHR) 95–96
Shah, Timothy Samuel 56
Shah of Iran 29 (box)
Shani, Giorgio 31, 76–77
sharia law 106
Shia Muslims (Shiites) 16
Singapore, Confucianism in 14
Snyder, Jack 8, 55, 57
social capital 39–41; development policies and 41; key aspect 41; relational characteristics of 40; religion leading source of 39; undermined 40
Social Contract, The (Rousseau) 79 (box)
Solidarity, support from Roman Catholic Church 70, 157
South-East Asia 12
South Korea: growth of Christianity 47 (box); relatively strong civil societies 38
Soviet Union 25; Cold War with USA 114; collapse of 46 (box), 49, 50, 156; invasion of Afghanistan 50
Spain: colonialism and 52 (box); 'generally religious'

state 30; 'third wave of democratisation' 33
Sri Lanka: Buddhist population 12; Hindu population 15
State: and church in France 25–26 (box); and civil religion in USA 23–24 (box); civil society 35–39; political society 32–35; social capital 39–41; theocratic revolution in Iran 29–30 (box)
Stepan, Alfred 23, 33, 37
stigmatisation of religious non-believers, Africa 126–127, 129–130
strong civil societies 38
Sudan 96; denial of rights of non-believers 128
Suharto, General 30
Sunnah 29 (box)
Sunni Muslims 16, 96, 97, 121, 128, 150, 151, 159, 162, 163, 164
Sustainable Development Goals 165
Sweden, strong civil society 38
Syria: sectarian divisions 121; state discrimination against Christian minorities 119

Taiwan: Buddhist population 12; Confucianism in 14; relatively strong civil societies 38
Talmud 17
Tanzania 128
Tarrow, Sidney 66 (box)
terrorism *see* 9/11; religious terrorism
Thailand, Buddhist population 12
theocracies 28, 46 (box)
Tibet 32; Buddhist population 12; China control of 32; Dalai Lama 11

Tilly, Charles 66 (box)
Tocqueville, Alexis de 79 (box)
Torah 17
Torpor, Lev 122
transformative minority politics 120 (box)
transnational business corporations (TNCs) 165
transnational Islamist *jihadist* groups, non-state religious actor 49
transnational networks, technological revolution and 51
transnationalism 54–55 (box)
Troy, Jodok 58
True, Jacqui 91
Trump, Donald 24 (box), 47 (box), 75, 77, 79 (box), 115, 123–124, 136–137, 145, 146, 147
trust 137 (box)
Tuksal, Hidayet 103–104
Tunisia 69; increased sectarian tensions 121
Turkey: Islamic feminism 102–104; Justice and Development Party (*Adalet ve Kalkınma Partisi;* AKP) 31, 76; multi-religious state 31; right-wing populism 75; state discrimination against Christian minorities 119

Uganda: denial of rights of non-believers 128; Humanist Association for Leadership Equality and Accountability (HALEA) 128; religion at public schools 129
United Kingdom, as 'post-secular' 59 (box)
United Nations (UN) 3; Christian conservative groups at 123–124 (box); Commission on the

Status of Women (CSW) 123 (box); Declaration on the Elimination of All Forms of Intolerance and Discrimination Based on Religion or Belief 114; gendered human rights 95; International Convention on Elimination of All Forms of Racial Discrimination 114; International Covenant on Civil and Political Rights (ICCPR) 113–114, 117; Minorities Declaration 117; sexual and reproductive health rights (SRHR) at 95–96 (box); Special Rapporteurs 114; Universal Declaration of Human Rights (UDHR) 113
United States of America (USA): anti-immigration stance 136–137; Christian Right 47 (box); civil religion and culture wars in 78–79 (box); civil religion and state in 23–24; civil religion in 30; Commission on International Religious Freedom (USCIRF) 115–116 (box), 119, 127; 'generally religious' state 30; growing interaction of religion and politics 46–47 (box); International Religious Freedom Act (IRFA) 115, 131n1; 'Mexico City policy' ('global gag rule') 123 (box); secular state 47 (box), 147

'unsecularization of the world' 53–54 (box)

Vietnam 32; Buddhist population 12; Confucianism in 14
Vietnam War 80
Virgin Mary 97–98
Vuola, Elina 97

Waever, Ole 75, 138
Wahhabism 150
Wald, Kenneth 78, 80–81, 147
Washington Consensus 41
Watergate scandal 80
weak civil societies 37–38
Weber, Max 144
Weigel, George 53–54 (box)
Welfare Party *(Refah Partisi)*, Turkey 31
Western Europe: immigration and 161–162; secularisation 161
Why Do People Discriminate against Jews (Fox) 122
Woodhead, Linda 93
World Bank 41, 92, 165
World Council of Churches 49, 165
world religions 10–17
World War II 2–3; international politics and religion after 46–47 (box); international religious freedom after 116–118; religious involvement in politics after 67

Yemen 166

For Product Safety Concerns and Information please contact our EU
representative GPSR@taylorandfrancis.com
Taylor & Francis Verlag GmbH, Kaufingerstraße 24, 80331 München, Germany

www.ingramcontent.com/pod-product-compliance
Lightning Source LLC
Chambersburg PA
CBHW050905160426
43194CB00011B/2292